49.7
Bel

Bell, A. Linnette   11/18
Making frames

DISCARDED

C000256965

MAKING
FRAMES

A. LINNETTE BELL

PERRY PUBLIC LIBRARY
PERRY, N.Y. 14530

THE CROWOOD PRESS

First published in 2018 by
The Crowood Press Ltd
Ramsbury, Marlborough
Wiltshire SN8 2HR

www.crowood.com

© A. Linnette Bell 2018

All rights reserved. No part of this publication may be reproduced or transmitted in any form or by any means, electronic or mechanical, including photocopy, recording, or any information storage and retrieval system, without permission in writing from the publishers.

British Library Cataloguing-in-Publication Data
A catalogue record for this book is available from the British Library.

ISBN 978 1 78500 395 0

Acknowledgements
Special thanks to Duncan McDonald and the team at All About Framing for their support and encouragement. To my husband David, for all his help with photography, computers and extreme patience in wading through the sea of creative clutter which has filled our home during the making of this book. To my mother June Bell, friends, customers, artists and students for providing artifacts to demonstrate framing methods and ideas. My thanks to Joseph McCarthy Fine Frames Ltd, and the many proof readers who have given their valuable feedback.

Typeset by Kelly-Anne Levey
Printed and bound in India by Replika Press Pvt Ltd

CONTENTS

INTRODUCTION

INSPIRATION

There will be a reason for leafing through the pages of this book. You may enjoy the challenge of designing bespoke framing and be looking for new and interesting ways to frame. By doing your own framing you can be sure that your artwork is framed to a good standard, or it may be a natural extension of the creative process of producing a piece of art. You may wish to save money, as the cost of quality framing can be expensive for the simple reason that the process can be time intensive, especially when it is of a more specialized type.

PRESENTATION

Framing is the finishing touch for presenting and if it's well designed and carried out correctly, will enhance and protect your artwork and precious items. The item to be framed might be linked to a hobby, or career as an artist or photographer. The perception of the value of artwork can also be affected by the framing. For example, when photographers enter their work for competition, it is usual to be marked down by the judges if mounts and frames are of poor quality, or the choice of framing is ill considered. You may want to present collectables or special events like sport, weddings, births and so on.

Traditional watercolour line and wash.

Random paint effect
using masking gum and
sponge paint effect.

Mount with a slip
on the inside edge

Double mount: top mount
with a painted bevel and
angled corners and bottom
mount with straight sides.
Artwork by the author.

STYLES AND FASHIONS

Manufacturers of mount board and moulding follow the current trends in the interior design industry, launching new mount board colours, moulding profiles and finishes now and then, while also supplying standard designs and colours that never go out of fashion. Popular interior design styles can be described as classical, modern, retro, shabby chic, art nouveau and art deco. The type of items or artwork to be framed can also be subject to changing fashions.

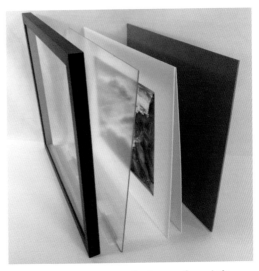

The basic components of a frame, from left to right: frame, glass, mounted artwork and backing board.

PROTECTION

The framing should not only complement the artwork and allow it to be seen without taking over due attention, it should be made using methods and materials that will preserve the contents. Picture framers from around the world have collectively established proven methods and materials for protecting valuable and fragile artwork and collectables. Presented here will be methods and materials recommended by the Fine Art Trade Guild (FATG).

FRAME CONSTRUCTION

In general, most frames will be constructed using a rigid outer wood, resin or metal frame with a rebate to hold glass, window mount and backing mount for containing the artwork and a rigid board behind to protect the back. The whole construction is generally held together with V nails, tabs or pins, tape and glue.

MODERN EQUIPMENT AND METHODS

This book presents the most convenient methods and latest equipment available. The availability of good-quality framing equipment has increased to the extent that some former methods of making mounts and frames now appear unnecessarily arduous.

LAYOUT OF THIS BOOK

This book will take you through the basic process, from measuring to assembly for framing paper-based artwork with alternatives for other types of artwork or collectables. Handy tips are highlighted along the way. It is intended as an overall introduction to framing that will hopefully give the reader encouragement to get started, or if they have some basic experience, the inspiration to try out some extra ideas, to add more flourish to their projects.

CHAPTER ONE

MATERIALS, TOOLS AND EQUIPMENT

GETTING STARTED

The huge range of materials and equipment required for framing can look daunting and expensive. However, with careful planning, you can buy just the basic necessities to get started and complete your first projects. A basic set of equipment includes a mount cutter, a saw and a joiner, plus consumable items like V nails and glue. Before purchasing equipment, many suppliers will demonstrate, and some will let you have hands-on experience, so that you know it is suitable for your particular needs. If you have limited space to store materials and equipment, some stages can be done for you. This might be cutting the moulding. For example, suppliers can offer a 45-degree mitre chop service, for which you must supply the correct glass size plus an extra 1–2mm on each side. Glass and mount should fit a little loosely in the frame, to allow for expansion and contraction. The chop service helps to avoid the accumulation of bits of moulding, and the need to store long lengths. By purchasing bare wood moulding and hand finishing with paint, dye or gilding as needed, which is explained in Chapter 10, you can minimize the accumulation of partly used lengths of finished moulding that may never be used. Glass cutting is another job that can be done for you, to avoid the danger of glass particles in areas where children and pets may be moving around.

WHEN BUYING GLASS CUT TO SIZE

Take your made-up frame along to the glass supplier and give it to them so they can measure and place the glass in the frame. Check before leaving the premises that there are no scratches or other marks on the glass and that it is cut to allow a little movement in case of contraction of wood in a warm room. The frame then serves as a support for transporting the glass safely.

If only the occasional circle or oval mount is needed, it may not be worth the expense of buying a specialist cutter for the purpose. A framer who leases a computerized mount cutter can create circles, ovals and other variations such as arches very quickly at a reasonable cost.

MATERIALS

Mount board

Mount board is generally composed of an inner pulp board covered with a front face of paper that can be either smooth or textured and a back face of plain paper. It is known as paper-faced board. Some mount boards are solid, with no layers for front and back. A range of colours, tones, tints and metallic finishes vary according to fashion but white, cream and black are constantly available. Mount board manufacturers usually give their mount colours descriptive names, evocative of current fashionable colours in the interior design industry. Manufacturers also produce a mount board with a colour core, most commonly a white or black mount board with a black core. When a bevel is cut, the result is a black line facing onto the artwork.

A code number is also given to each colour, which can be found on the back of paper-faced mount board. You will need to look hard for it on mount board with a black core, as that side will be almost black. Different qualities of mount board are described as standard, conservation and cotton museum by the Fine Art Trade Guild (FATG).

Double mount with black core. Lake Windermere photograph by the author.

Standard mount board

Standard mount board is the least expensive and is available in a wide range of colours. The core will become brown after a while, as the board becomes acidic, due to the lignin in the wood pulp from which it is made. Acid from a standard mount will leach into the framed artwork and cause unsightly brown marks, known as foxing, making it unsuitable for framing artwork of value.

A selection of colours with black core.

Conservation mount board

Conservation mount board is treated to remove the lignin, so the core remains white. It is widely available in a good range of colours and is suitable for most projects.

Museum mount board

Museum mount board is the best quality and the most expensive, made from 100 per cent cotton rag. The colour range is fairly limited and not all suppliers carry it in stock. It is recommended (FATG) for high-value artwork, or museum exhibits.

Mount board is available in various thicknesses, which are commonly measured in microns. A micron is equal to 1 millimetre (FATG). It is

A selection of mount board colours.

available from 900 microns up to 3,500 microns. Conservation grade mount board is usually around 1,100 to 1,400 microns thick and up to 3,500 microns in a few colours.

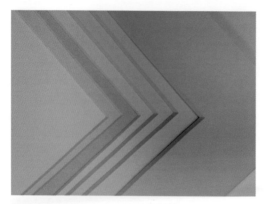

Mount board in a variety of thicknesses.

White archival gummed tape, pH-neutral self-adhesive tape, linen hinging tape, brown gummed tape, brown self-adhesive picture tape.

Tapes

Basic tapes needed for picture framing are archival white gummed tape for fixing artwork into a mount, and a brown picture tape, which is available as gummed or self adhesive, for finishing the back of the frame. For artwork of an insignificant value, a self-adhesive pH-neutral white tape is all right for fixing into a mount, but it is the only type of sticky tape that should be used. Sellotape, masking tape or any other sticky tape will cause irreparable damage by leaving stains and a sticky mess. Sello tape and masking tape also eventually dry out, allowing the artwork to drop out of the mount.

Moulding

The range of moulding designs is vast, and potentially bewildering to the new framer. Manufacturers compete with each other to produce ever more unique patterns. As each style is copyrighted, it is not possible to buy the exact same moulding from a different manufacturer. Watch out for lookalike mouldings with slightly different dimensions as this might be how they have imitated another manufacturer's shape without infringing a copyright. They often give a range of moulding names which follow the latest interior design styles, though each moulding will have a manufacturer's or supplier's code for reference.

It is possible to design and make your own moulding, to create a very exclusive appearance to your framing. Some manufacturers will make bare wood moulding to your design for a minimum order, or anyone who can use a bench-mounted router can make a moulding for you.

A feature unique to all moulding is the depth of rebate. It is most often the reason why a particular moulding is chosen. It will be important to see if the glass, mounts and backing board are going to fit into the rebate space. The lip rebate is the inside edge that comes in front of the glass and mount, which holds all the components of the frame together.

Though moulding shapes and finishes change with fashion, it is possible to classify some basic moulding shapes as flat, cushion, hockey stick, reverse bevel, spoon, cassetta, pasta and tray, which might make your selection easier.

Flat, cushion and hockey stick mouldings are good for a minimalist or modern style effect. Reverse bevels look good on bold, single-item images that appear to be very close, while spoon-shaped moulding is effective in leading the eye inwards into an image with pictorial depth, and is often used for traditional landscapes. A cassetta is an elegant classical, Italian style with a flat middle and raised pattern on either side. Pasta is made of wood powder and glue and pressed into

Moulding shapes include: Flat, hockey stick, reverse bevel, spoon, tray or inlay, cassetta and pasta.

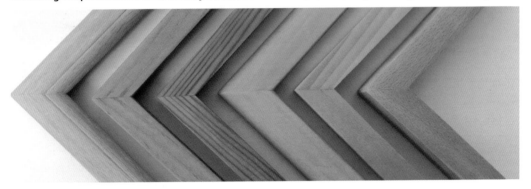

From left: Oak, ash, pine, obeche, tulip, beech.

CHOOSING AND BUYING MOULDING

For your first few projects, select a moulding shape that will be easy to join, such as flat, and which will remain stable when a V nail is inserted into the back.

Before buying moulding check that it isn't warped in any direction by holding one end towards your eye, looking down to the other end. Any warps or twists in any direction will be visible. Warped moulding will not join neatly and the resulting frame may not sit flat, causing gaps to open in the corners when glass, mount and backing board are put in.

Rebates (Rabbets)

Rebate (rabbet) depth and rebate lip.

raised patterns onto a wood base. It is available in a variety of patterns and is perfect for adding gilding and paint effects. Tray, sometimes known as inlay, is a modern style especially suited to framing stretched canvas. The canvas is placed in the frame from the front and screwed to the frame from the back. There is no rebate lip to cover the edges of the canvas so the whole image is in full view.

Moulding that can be cut by a framer is made from a range of wood types or plastic resin. Woods are classified as either hard or soft. Some examples of hard woods are oak, ash, beech and obeche. Obeche is a large tropical tree from West Africa. Although it is physically not hard, it is classified as such because it has a close and uniform grain. Along with pine it is now one of the

From top: Fillets of various size, slips in various shapes and a slip with gilt finish.

From top: 15mm, 12mm, 10mm, 7mm and 5mm deep V nails.

most commonly used types of wood for picture framing. Many obeche bare wood mouldings are available, which are perfect for decorative painting and gilding. Pine is a soft wood and the grain can be an attractive feature, although wood knots and resin can be a problem.

Slips and fillets

Slips are thin decorative additions than can be placed inside the main moulding for extra width or inside the mount window. Sometimes they are covered with canvas, velvet or linen as a contrast to the finish on the moulding.

A fillet is a spacer bar for creating distance between the artwork and the glass. It is essentially needed when a mount is not desired, to prevent the glass from touching the artwork and transferring moisture.

Wood glue

For applying to the 45-degree mitres before fixing together with V nails. Ordinary white PVA wood glue is sufficient for adding extra stability to the join, particularly towards the front face of the moulding. The V nail won't reach the last quarter to one third of the height.

V nails or wedges

V shaped metal wedges designed for use in a hand-operated joiner or foot-operated underpinner are a quick and convenient way of fixing a frame together. They are usually taped together as a flexible ribbon ready for loading into a foot-operated underpinner and have a sharp cutting end, which drives into the moulding. Some manufacturers supply them in a cartridge designed to fit their particular model of foot-operated underpinner. The V nail is available in various heights, such as 5mm, 7mm, 10mm, 12mm and 15mm. Select a V nail which is about three quarters of the height of your moulding. Different V nails are often described as being suitable for either hard or soft wood.

Glass and acrylic glass

Standard glass for picture framing is 2mm thick float glass. It can be scored and snapped apart easily using a hand-held glass cutter. If glare from lamps or windows is a problem, non-reflective glass may help to reduce the reflection. Non-reflective glass has been etched on one or both sides to give a matt surface. It is suitable for framing paper-based subjects which require just a single mount, as greater distance between glass and image will reduce clarity. It is generally about twice the cost of standard glass.

Acrylic glass may be a preferable option, as it will reduce the final weight of the frame; allow the frame to be posted without breakage; or allow safe use in a child's bedroom. Acrylic glass is also available as non reflective. When using acrylic glass, don't forget to remove the protective plastic sheeting from both sides, after scoring and snapping it. This is best done just before assembling, as acrylic glass attracts dust due to static electricity.

A superior range of glass with special coatings that keep out 90 per cent of ultraviolet rays, or which is virtually invisible because it doesn't reflect, is available at about six times the cost of standard glass. Presently these speciality glasses are being used more commonly as standard in the picture framing industry.

Backing board

Backing board is the final protective board at the back of the picture frame. It is rigid for strength, mostly brown in colour and can be easily cut with a sharp craft knife. It should not be a tight fit in the frame, but allow about 1mm all round for possible expansion or contraction of the frame. For a frame that needs a backing board larger than the size that is available, good quality hardboard or thin ply from a DIY store will be adequate. It is worth getting the store to cut it to size if possible for a neat edge.

From left: Brown craft board, ply board, cords, wire, strap fittings, D-rings, bendable metal plates, turn key, corner braces, self-tapping screws and bumpers.

Fixings, cord, wire and bumpers

D-rings and self-tapping screws are commonly used for their neat appearance, as they lie flat against the frame. They are available in three sizes. For narrow frames use small, wider frames use medium, and for larger, heavier frames, a large or double-D with two screw holes. For very heavy frames long strap fittings are safer, as a D-ring may split apart under the weight.

Nylon cord in a variety of thicknesses and breaking strengths, chosen according to the weight of the frame, is commonly used. The weight of the frame should be no more than a fifth of the breaking strength of the cord. Metal cord made of brass is available if preferred and has a more aesthetic look, especially if the picture is to be hung from a picture rail and it will be in view from the front. For seaside locations, a non-corroding wire made from stainless steel, silver in colour is advised. Picture wire is available with a clear plastic coating to make the wiring process easier.

Bumpers are adhesive pads made of felt or cork, which are applied to the bottom corners of a frame to hold it away from the wall so that air can circulate behind it.

SPECIALITY MATERIALS

Brushes, rag and sponge

Brushes
A range of brushes is needed for preparation of surfaces as well as application of paint and

Soft pastels, rag, sponges, masking tape, art masking fluid, gold ink, acrylic paints, artists' watercolour paint, designers' gouache, brushes and lining pens.

From left: Mount bevel decoration tape, double-sided easy-lift tape, spray glue, Scotch 811 removable sticky tape, high tack spray glue, archival mounting strips, Mighty Mounts, miniature cable ties, mounting corners and clear archival polyester.

gilding onto frames. A wire brush is used for brushing the surface of bare wood to open the grain ready for applying liming wax. Artists' watercolour brushes are used for painting broad areas of wash for mount decoration. A bristle sash brush is needed for applying gesso and size to a bare wood moulding and a soft hair brush for applying coloured bole and varnish. A nylon brush is sufficient for applying wood dyes straight onto a bare wood moulding. Wonderful paint effects can be achieved with a toothbrush, or a worn-out artists' hog bristle brush.

Rag and sponge
Soft cotton rag and natural sponge can be used to create special paint effects on a prepared bare wood moulding.

Artists' watercolour paint, designers gouache and soft pastel

Artists' quality fade-resistant watercolour paints are for decorative effects on mount windows and for use in a wash lining pen. Designers' gouache is an opaque water-based paint, which can be used in a lining pen for a bolder effect. Soft pastel can be powdered onto masked-off areas on mount board.

Artists' acrylic paints

Tubes of artists' paint for creating paint effects on window mounts and moulding. They dry fast, which is an advantage for applying layers of different colour.

Speciality tapes and glue

Removable sticky tape or masking tape

Removable sticky tape (such as Scotch 811) is for masking areas on the front of the mount board for adding a painted decorative effect. It can be removed easily without damaging the surface.

Double-sided tape

Used for taping two flat surfaces together. Finger-lift double-sided tape is easier to use.

Mount and bevel decoration tape

Used for creating deep bevels, it is available in a range of colours.

Glue

As a spray or paste for mount decoration and fixing fabric to mount board.

Wood dyes

Water-based wood dyes are the easiest to use. Brushes for applying dye can be washed out in water. If hard wood mouldings such as ash, beech or oak are to be dyed, a spirit-based dye will be needed. Brushes will need to be cleaned in white spirit. Spirit dye has a very strong odour, so those who are sensitive might rather avoid it, or at least use it in a well-ventilated area. Overalls are recommended to protect clothing when using dye and acrylic paints.

Wood waxes

After a dye has been applied, a wood moulding needs sealing. Applying a coat of wax is a quick and easy method. Waxes are available as clear, or in various wood colours.

Liming wax

A white wax made of lime and paraffin wax, which is very easy to apply and creates the distinctive limed wax look, which gives textural detail to wood grain. Looks best on oak, but can be used to create an effect on other types of wood. Liming wax has a strong odour and when applying it, the use of thin, disposable plastic gloves is recommended for anyone with sensitive skin.

Rabbit-skin glue

Animal glue used to bind whiting to make gesso and to size a bare wood moulding before applying gesso. It can be purchased from a framing supplier, or an art material supplier. The granular form of glue is easily dissolved in a little warm water and heated gently in a bain-marie or double saucepan to make a thin liquid glue.

From left: Liming wax, wire brush, wood waxes, fine grade sand paper, wood dyes, disposable gloves and rag.

Gesso

It is used for creating a smooth, even surface on bare wood moulding in preparation for gilding. It can be purchased ready made, but it is better made fresh as required. It is made of whiting and rabbit-skin glue.

Clay bole

It is used to give a rich effect under real gold leaf gilding, or imitation metal leaf. Different coloured clays are used for different purposes. For example, red clay is used under real gold leaf because it looks especially rich with gold and is suitable for burnishing to a shine. Clay bole can be purchased ready made but it is also better made fresh as required. The clay can be purchased in one piece, which needs to be grated into a powder and mixed with a little rabbit-skin glue.

Gold, silver and metal leaf

To create a beautiful, unique shiny finish on bare wood moulding, real gold, silver or imitation gold and silver are needed. Thin leaves of metal are available in small, square sheets, or on a roll. Leaf that has been pressed onto wax paper, known as transfer, is much easier to handle, especially for applying to broad areas, but loose-leaf sheets are needed for gilding in nooks and crannies as on a classical swept design.

Acrylic glue size and Japan gold size

Acrylic glue size is a convenient modern size for applying metal leaf. As a little goes a long way, a small bottle will last for ages. For oil gilding, Japan gold size is needed. Winsor and Newton make a Japan gold size with a short drying time.

From left: Whiting, sash brush, rabbit-skin granules, yellow and red clay bole, gilders' cushion, knife, real gold leaf, gilding brush, agate burnishers, metal flakes, aluminium silver and metal leaf in sheets and a roll, rottenstone, Japan size, Wundersize acrylic size, gilt cream, gilt varnish, nylon gloves and varnish brushes.

Varnishes

Used for sealing imitation metal leaf to prevent oxidization, or to make final adjustments to the colour by adding a little pigment. For a permanent surface, Japan gold size can be used as a varnish. It is applied with a soft brush, which can be cleaned with white spirit.

Rottenstone

A grey mineral powder that creates an aged, antique effect when dusted into the crevices of a classical swept frame or pasta moulding.

TOOLS AND EQUIPMENT

Paperweight and magnifier

Dome-shaped glass paperweights will hold down curly artwork without damage and magnify areas for closer inspection.

Sharp pencil

A sharp HB pencil is needed for marking borders on the back of the mount board before cutting.

Clean eraser

A clean eraser is needed for removing pencil lines on the back of the mount board, after cutting. To clean any marks that accidentally appear on the front, use a putty rubber to lift out the mark without damaging the surface.

Bone paper folder

For smoothing down any raised corners on a mount after the window has been cut and for folding white archival gummed tape when making hinges for attaching artwork.

Metal rulers, T square and squaring arm

A metal ruler which starts from zero and with millimetre increments will help to save time when measuring mount board, as the ruler can be easily lined up to the edge by touch. Use a 60cm (24 inches) or 1 meter (40 inches) and 15cm (6 inches) for small jobs. A T square or squaring arm is useful for checking that the corners of mount board are a perfect 45 degrees and for cutting glass.

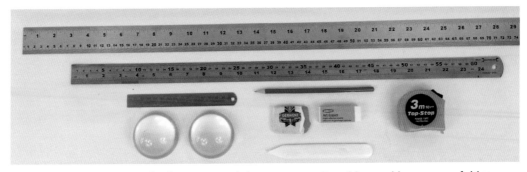

Rulers, tape measure, pencil, glass paperweights, eraser, putty rubber and bone paper folder.

Notepaper or planning sheet

For keeping a record of measurements as you work through each stage of a framing project. It can save time, and could form a useful record for repeating the same idea later.

Calculator and tape measure

A calculator is useful for working out how much mount board and moulding to buy along with a 3-metre (10ft) metal tape measure for checking moulding lengths.

Mount cutter

A mount cutter can be a simple ruler with rubber beading on the underneath to grip a prepared cutting surface and include a rail for a hand-held mount cutter head to slide along. This simple mount cutter is available in various lengths. It is easy to store, as it takes up very little space. Because the rubber beading both grips and

raises the edge of the ruler, it can also be used for cutting glass and drawing watercolour lines on mount board.

A mount-cutting rule that is mounted onto a board will give more stability, and may have some extra features, such as start and stop gauges, a border marker and a scaled right-angle arm, which aids in measuring and cutting an accurate 90-degree corner. Board-mounted cutters are available in various lengths. They may be fixed so that the mount board slides between the rail and the board, or with a hinge, which allows the cutter to be opened for easy insertion of the mount board.

A board-mounted cutter kit generally will include two cutters. A bevel, or slanted cutter head which slopes down toward the artwork being mounted and a straight cutter for cutting the outside edges of the mount board. The bevel cutter head is either pushed away or pulled towards the operator. Even pressure is achieved when using a mount-cutting head that is pulled towards you, as the mount is pulled into the corner of the mount cutter. As a push-style mount cutter head moves forward, it is necessary to prevent the mount from moving as it is cut. Additionally, a pull-style cutter may be easier for a left-handed user.

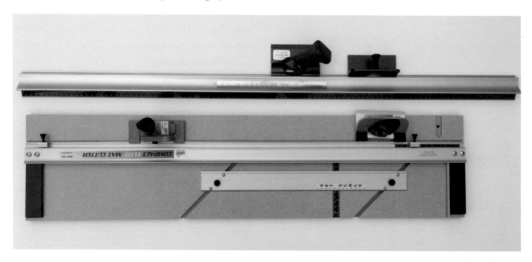

A simple mount cutter with straight and bevel cutting heads and a mount cutter mounted on a board.

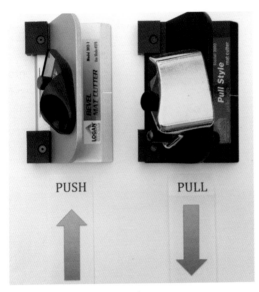

PUSH   PULL

Push style cutter, pull style cutter.

**Logan Platinum Edge mat cutter.
(Photo: Logan Graphic Products, Inc. USA.)**

If space and cost are not an issue, for about twice the cost of a large board-mounted cutter, a more professional cutter will offer some useful extra features, such as a dual-headed cutter, which changes angles at the flick of a switch and which will generally be a much heftier machine made of stronger quality materials to stand up to frequent use.

Blades

Mount-cutter blades are rectangular and for most cutters are designed to be turned round, so that both corners are used, leaving the centre still sharp. When blades are not designed to be turned around, they are only sharpened on one side, which allows for a more stable cut because the blade will not bend. They are designed for use in a combined straight and bevel cutter system.

Saw blades are available for sawing hard and soft wood and will need replacing when worn out. Mitre trimmer blades and mitre guillotine blades can be re-sharpened, which must be done by a professional.

Mitre saw

A good-quality saw will make mitre cuts accurate enough to fit together without gaps. There are 45-degree markers on each side, which click when the saw is lined up to them. Only one mitre can be sawn at a time. There are usually drill holes to attach the saw to a bench for stability and adjustable clamps to hold the moulding in place. A gauge on the measuring arm will allow the user to cut a second piece of moulding to the same length. Moulding with a maximum width of about 10cm (4 inches) can be cut on a mitre saw.

UPCYCLING OLD FRAMES

Old frames often contain hidden nails, which will irretrievably damage a blade that hits them, therefore it is not recommended to cut them down with a mitre cutter or mitre guillotine. Replacement blades for both the mitre cutter and mitre guillotine are expensive.

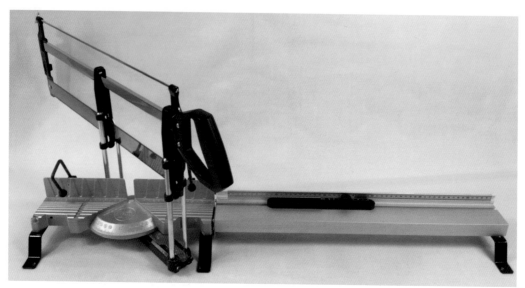

Mitre saw with measuring system.

Mitre guillotine

If space and cost are not an issue, a foot-operated mitre guillotine will speed up the process
by allowing two mitres to be cut at a time. The
moulding is placed in the guillotine with rebate
facing away from the operator and two supports
are placed under the rebate to prevent it from
being broken off by the heavy downward action
of the blades. The moulding is cut in small stages
as the blades are moved forwards by the action
of a lever. There are two calibrations to calculate
the position of the gauge according to width of
moulding and length needed. Moulding with a
maximum width of about 9cm (3½ inches) can
be cut on a mitre guillotine.

Mitre trimmer

This is a fine finishing tool with a gentler action
than a saw or guillotine, as it slices sideways. It
cannot replace a saw or mitre guillotine as only
very thin shavings on each 45-degree mitre
can be cut. However, the mitres will fit per-

fectly together. It is especially useful for gilt-
finished mouldings that are liable to chip, or
some bare woods such as obeche, whose fibres
can sometimes tear or crush easily under the
weight of guillotine blades.

Underpinner or joiner

Underpinners are foot-operated tools designed
to drive V nails into the corners on the back of
the frame. A joiner is a hand-operated pinner
using a single V nail which is held in place on
a magnetic post with its sharp cutting end facing down towards the frame, then a lever action
forces the V nail down into the wood. The moulding is held together by either a corner clamp or
a strap clamp while the pinning is in progress.
The hand-operated version is a simple yet reli-
able tool, worth keeping even if you decide later
to upgrade to the faster foot-operated machine.
The hand lever is either mounted on one post,
or a bar between two posts. The one-post design
can pin wide moulding.

Mitre trimmer and optional measuring gauge.

VMM Guillotine. (Photo: Charnwood, UK)

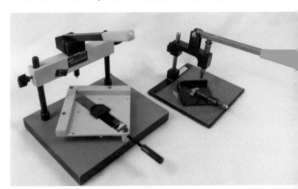

Hand-operated joiners with single and double posts and clamps.

The features of a foot-operated underpinner include a shaft or V nail holder, which accepts a long ribbon of V nails taped together along the sharp cutting end, a rebate support bar, and stop screws to set positions for inserting two V nails.

Glass cutter, glass nippers, acrylic glass scorer, glass marker pen and glass cleaner

Technically a glass cutter is a scorer, rather than a cutter. It is a small metal wheel, which must be kept lubricated to create a score, which with gentle pressure allows the glass to snap apart. Some features to look for include a reservoir for instant lubrication, a weighted cutting head for making a strong score, and a metal ball on the handle for tapping along a score prior to snapping. Glass cutters are mostly shaped like a pen, or they may be designed to glide on a mount cutter rail for extra stability.

An acrylic glass scorer is a hand-held tool with a sharp blade for making a score in acrylic glass, which is then snapped apart.

A glass marker pen is a pen designed to mark scoring positions on glass. The marks can be removed later with glass cleaner.

Glass nippers, shaped like a pair of pliers, are used to hold onto and snap off long thin pieces of glass.

A good-quality quick-drying glass cleaner and a lint-free cloth are needed to clean the glass of smears and dust both sides before assembling the contents of the frame.

Safety goggles and glass gloves

Safety goggles ensure that small shards of glass won't enter the eyes when snapping the glass. Glass gloves have a rubber side that covers the palm of the hand, to allow for non-slip, safe handling of glass.

**Alfamacchine U200 manual underpinner.
(Photo: Alfamacchine, Italy)**

**From left: Glass-handling gloves, safety
goggles, lint-free cloth, glass cleaner, glass
cutter lubrication oil, glass cutter, glass nippers,
glass marker pen, acrylic glass scorer.**

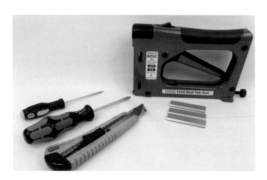

Bradawl, screwdriver, craft knife, tab gun and tabs.

Tab gun, panel pins, tabs

A tab gun is a hand tool for firing metal tabs or
points into the rebate at the back of the frame,
to hold the glass, mount and backing board
inside. Flexible tabs, which can be bent open
with fingers, will allow for easy opening of the
frame for dust removal but to finish, rigid tabs or
pins are necessary for greater strength.

Screwdriver

Cross-head screwdriver for screwing self-tapping
screws into the back of the frame, for holding
D-rings or strap fasteners in place.

Bradawl

A hand tool with a sharp point for piloting holes
in soft wood to accept a self-tapping screw.

Cordless electric drill
and screwdriver

For screwing self-tapping screws into hard wood
such as ash, beech or oak.

Craft knife

Will be needed for cutting tape, cord and trimming. Choose a sturdy knife with a retractable
blade.

SPECIALITY TOOLS

Oval or circle mount cutter

A basic oval-to-circle mount cutter is an oval-shaped tool with a rotating measuring arm and blade holder. It adjusts easily from a circle to an oval by loosening a centre knob and sliding the scale arm.

Oval and circular mount cutter, mount corner marker, foam core cutters, embossing tool set.

Foam core cutter

For making deep bevel decoration on mounts, a special cutting tool is needed for cutting foam core at an angle or straight. The cutter blade can be adjusted to cut foam core of 3mm; 5mm or 10mm thickness.

Deep bevel mount cutters.

Corner marker

A useful tool for marking starting points in the corners of a mount for applying traditional line wash or other types of decoration, or for marking the starting points for an embossing tool. The tool has a measuring scale with corresponding holes for marking the mount with a light pencil mark, or sharp point.

Line marker pen and brush

For making traditional, decorative watercolour lines and applying broad areas of colour. It has an adjustable nib, which holds a small amount of dilute watercolour. A good quality pen will be able to hold enough liquid to make a clean, continuous line along each side of the mount.

Embossing tool

For making a decorative embossed groove around the mount. It is a set of hand tools with three sizes of metal ball and a sharp point for marking the corners.

Deep bevel mount cutter

A deep bevel mount cutter is a specially made tool for cutting bevels in thicker mount board such as 2mm (2,000 microns) and 3.5mm (3 sixteenths of an inch or 3,500 microns). Alternatively, the blade on a professional level mount cutter can be adjusted to cut thicker mount board.

MEASURING

PREPARATION AND CARE

Some artwork will need preparation. For example, if it is received in a postal tube, it will need to be flattened between two clean mount boards under weights. Oil or acrylic paintings and also some prints can be on canvas, which may need stretching prior to framing. The surplus canvas

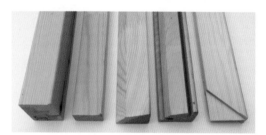

From left: Heavy weight stretcher bar moulding, light weight, two-way stretchable moulding and ready-made stretcher bar.

Slotting stretcher bars together.

around the image will determine how deep the stretcher bar should be. Usual stretcher depths are 18mm, (¾ inch), 25mm (1 inch) and 40mm (1½ inches). Stretchers are available pre-cut to standard sizes that slot together, or as lengths of wood, like moulding, which can be cut to any size. There needs to be enough canvas to go down the side and to the back, where it will be stretched and stapled. Some canvases will have been removed from a stretcher for easier transporting. Check that the artist has used a true rectangle by measuring diagonally from corner to corner. Stretched artwork will not require a mount or glass.

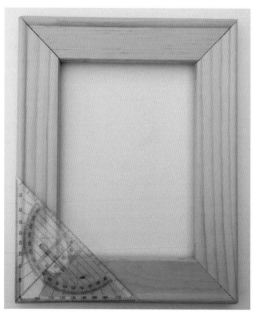

Squaring the stretcher.

Signed print mounted with space around the edges. Artwork by the author.

If the artwork is a delicate item that can smudge, like a soft pastel or charcoal drawing, leave it laid out flat, with nothing on top. Care is also needed when removing plastic wrapping as sticky tape can easily cause damage. Handle the artwork with clean, dry hands and place on a clean and dry work surface. Artwork should not be trimmed around the edges without permission from the owner.

Squaring the canvas over the stretcher.

CALCULATING HOW MUCH MOUNT BOARD AND MOULDING TO BUY

To estimate the amount of mount board you need, use the outside board measurement, that is artwork size plus twice the planned border width. Two boards this size are needed for each item to be framed, or three for a double mount. Mount board is available in sheets 1,120mm by 815mm (44 by 32 inches). It is also available as jumbo size 1,630mm by 1,120mm (64 by 44 inches) in a limited range of colours.

To calculate how much moulding to buy, use the outside board measurement and add on an extra 1–2mm for each side. Add the four side measurements together and add on eight times the width of the moulding. Finally, add 20 per cent to allow for any blemishes and wastage. Round the figure up to the lengths available. However, even if 2 metres (7ft) is all that is needed in your choice of moulding, the supplier may supply as much as 3 metres (10ft) as a minimum.

Moulding is sold in lengths of 2 metres (7ft), 2½ metres (8ft), 2¾ metres (9ft) or 3 metres (10ft).

Stretching and stapling.

Folding the corners of the canvas.

Measuring the window size for the artwork. Measuring horizontally at the top and bottom, vertically, both sides.

MEASURING THE ARTWORK

Begin the process of framing by measuring the artwork. These measurements will determine the mount, glass, backing board and frame sizes needed. It is necessary to check if standard sizes of each of the components can be used, or if jumbo or other alternatives will be needed. For large frames, it is important to choose a wider, sturdier moulding that won't bow out in the middle, causing the contents to come out of the frame. If the glazing required is larger than the size of the largest available sheet of glass, it may be necessary to order acrylic glass or 3mm thick glass cut to size. The frame will need to be very sturdy to be able to support the extra weight of 3mm thick glass.

The artwork is measured across the top and across the bottom because items may not be squared, particularly paintings and some prints. If the artwork is extremely out of true, it is a good idea to measure across the centre as well. If the image covers the entire paper, a minimum of 2–3mm is taken off the measurement each side so that the artwork does not fall through the mount window. It will be easier to mount larger artwork if a larger allowance of 5mm (¼ inch) to 10mm (½ inch) is used.

For an image that does not go all the way to the edge of the paper, it is not necessary to trim, just leave the extra paper behind the mount border. If you want to trim more off the image, for example part of a photograph may not be required, instead of cutting the photograph, the unwanted areas can be hidden behind the mount. It may be necessary to increase the width of the mount to conceal the hidden area, especially if the artwork is precious and cutting it may affect its value. When measuring the window opening for a print or etching that has been signed and given a limited edition number under the image, allow some extra space around the sides and top as well for a balanced, spacious effect.

These measurements will be the window size. Jot them down on paper, ready for the next stage.

MEASURING THE MOUNT

The next stage is to decide how wide to have the mount. It will be easier to get an overall idea of how the finished project will look if you line a small sample of the mount on the left-hand corner of the artwork and place a sample of the frame moulding on top with the sight edge facing towards the artwork. Move the moulding sample towards the artwork and back away to vary the width of mount showing. Stand back and find the most pleasing width. There are no

QUICK METHOD FOR MEASURING

Place a steel ruler that starts from zero about 2–3mm in from the left edge of the artwork and read off on the right side about 2–3mm inside the artwork. Then do the same on the vertical sides. It saves time over taking the whole measurement and then subtracting the amount needed to prevent the artwork from falling through the window.

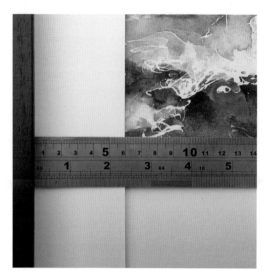

Planning the border width of the window mount.

Adding twice the border width to the window size to determine the outside board measurement.

rules about the mount width to the moulding width, except it is a good idea to avoid making a stripy effect by making the mount width the same width as the moulding.

ALTERNATIVE MOUNT STYLES

Sometimes the width of the mount can be made different on one or two of the four sides for effect.

Weighted mount

When composing a piece of artwork, the first consideration for an artist or photographer is to place a horizon line, or eye level. In simple terms, this means the line where the sky meets the land. If this line is in the middle, or the bottom third of the image it is usual to add extra width to the bottom border to compensate, otherwise the image will look top heavy. Around 5mm (¼ inch) or more, depending on how low the horizon line is, can be added to the bottom border to weight the mount. Another reason for making a weighted mount is that it will allow some extra space for an artist's signature, in particular for photographs, which cannot be signed on the actual artwork.

Museum mount

This style is a much deeper version of the weighted mount. It is often used for museum exhibits.

Wider sides

Wider borders on both sides can give the appearance that the image is stretching out horizontally.

Wider at the top and bottom

Extra wide all round

When the top and bottom are wider than the sides, the image has the appearance of stretching vertically.

An extra-wide mount is a helpful way of giving a small piece of artwork greater significance.

An extra-wide border at the bottom balances a low horizon line in this photograph of the Thames by the author.

An acrylic with extra-wide side borders. The height of a tin mine is accentuated with extra width at the top and bottom. Cow in museum mount. Small leaf print in an extra-wide mount. Artwork by the author.

Leaf prints on deckle edge watercolour paper float mounted and shadow float mounted.

Float mounting and shadow float mounting

Sometimes an artwork looks better without an overlapping mount. It may be an irregular shape, or the edges have a decorative effect, such as deckle edge paper. For float mounting it will be attached to a mount board, and a larger window mount cut to leave a gap all round it. Shadow float mounting is similar, but with some extra depth, as the artwork is mounted on foam core or other suitable material to give the effect of floating in space.

These styles need a moulding with a deep rebate and some fillet to separate the glass from the artwork.

and bottom measurements must be added to the height measurement of the window size. The sums of each of these measurements will give the dimensions of the boards needed. For accuracy, place a ruler along the edge of the back of the mount board and make a mark at the top and the bottom. Cut all the way across using a straight cutter. Then mark top and bottom for the other measurement and cut across. This process will need to be repeated as two boards are needed, one for the window itself, and one for attaching the artwork. It can be done much faster using a mount cutter with a squaring arm with a measuring scale. Save any long strips of mount board, as they will be needed later.

CUTTING TWO BOARDS, ONE EACH FOR THE WINDOW AND THE BACKING

Once the border widths have been decided, they can be added to the window size needed for the artwork jotted down earlier. The two side measurements must be added to the width measurement of the window size, and the top

MARKING THE BORDERS

The borders can be marked out on the back of just one of the two prepared mount boards in one of three ways.

If you are using a basic rule-style mount cutter, the borders can be marked by hand or by using a border marker, which holds a pencil. If a board-mounted cutter is being used, there will be an integral border gauge with a scale that can be set to the width needed. Then a pencil line is drawn where the cutting rail comes on

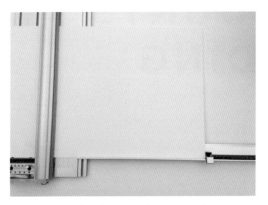

Using a mount cutter that has a squaring arm to measure and cut mount board.

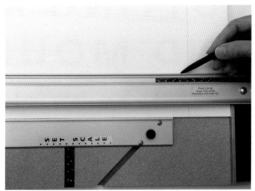

Using a measuring gauge to measure and mark the borders for a 6cm (2½ inch) wide border.

the mount board. A professional mount cutter will have border width gauges which can be set ready to cut without marking with a pencil.

CHECKING THE WINDOW SIZE

Once the border has been marked out, place the artwork on top of the pencil lines to check that the window is the right size before cutting.

Checking that the artwork will fit the window mount before cutting.

SINK MOUNT METHOD FOR ARTWORK OF BOARD THICKNESS

If the artwork is thicker than paper, it will need a sink mount, as a space between the window mount and backing board will be created that needs to be filled. A border is made using either mount board or foam core to place around the artwork as it is laid out on the backing board. This border may need to be kept in place with double-sided tape. The window mount is then placed on top and will remain flat.

Using foam core to create a sink mount. Cross stitch by Heritage Crafts Ltd. from a painting by John Clayton.

CUTTING MOUNTS AND MOULDING

CUTTING THE WINDOW MOUNT

Using a slip mat (spare strip of mount board)

For all mount cutters, a slip mat – which is just a narrow piece of mount board about 15cm (6 inches) wide – will protect a work surface, or the board on a board-mounted cutter, and will help to achieve a smooth, clean cut. Place the board previously marked out with pencil lines with the front

Placing the mount board in the mount cutter.

Changing blades.

facing down on top of the slip mat. Plan to cut the longer sides of the window first. The pencil lines will be in view and they are then lined up with the ruler edge of the mount cutter. The lining-up position is that which is made by a pencil when held at an angle to draw a line against a straight edge.

Mount cutter blade check

Before cutting, always check the blade is sharp and that the corners are not chipped. As a rough guide, you may be able to cut between ten and twenty mounts with each blade, but that will depend on the size of mount and also the type of mount board. Some mount boards wear blades out faster than others. If the cut is not smooth and the corners uneven, suspect the blade; it most likely needs replacing, or turn it around and use the other corner if it is a two-sided blade. Some mount cutter heads feature a blade slot, which keeps a double-sided blade straight while cutting. Care must be taken that the blade is placed in the slot before cutting. Always remember it is more economical to replace a blade than a sheet of mount board.

Start and stop positions

Some mount-cutting heads have a small line indicating the position to start and stop the cut. After placing the cutter on its rail, this mark is lined up with the pencilled border to cut a perfect corner without over- or under-cuts.

Some board-mounted cutters have small start and stop gauges that can be tightened against the cutter while it is being lined up. The gauge prevents an accidental under- or over-cut. Another feature that some mount cutters may have is a right-angle bar, which ensures that the mount board is squarely positioned in the mount cutter. The mount board should be placed accurately against the right-angle bar and the border width-measuring gauge, which is set on the desired width.

Push-style mount cutter

If you are using a push-style mount cutter, start from the right and line the small line on the cutter up with the pencil border. Keeping the cutter still, lever the blade down until it cuts into the mount board. The cutting mat and mount board can easily move when using the cutter so it is a good idea to place a hand on the mount to prevent movement as the mount cutter is pushed forward until the small line is even with the pencil border on the other side. The blade is raised and the opposite side of the window mount can be cut, for which the stop gauge is already positioned. The gauge will then need adjusting to cut the two smaller sides of the window mount.

Pull-style mount cutter

The stop gauge needs to be set up on the right side against the mount cutter head once it has been aligned, so that the mark lines up with the pencil line. Starting from the left, the blade is levered in to the mount board and the cutter is pulled towards the operator.

Perfecting mount window corners

If despite all precautions the corners have lifted, they can be smoothed down with a bone paper folder.

WHAT TO DO WITH THE LEFTOVER MOUNT BOARD

After cutting the mount board, you will have offcuts and the centre piece from the window mount which is known as a 'fall-out'. Pencil the mount name on the back of usable pieces and store in a wrapper, away from damp and light. Trim the fallout bevel edges to a straight edge and set aside long, thin lengths of board for use as cutting mats.

Lining up the mark on the mount cutter with the pencil line, to prevent under- or over-cuts. Using start and stop gauges to prevent the cutting head from slipping backwards or over-cutting.

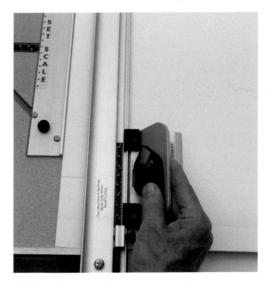

Cutting the mount.

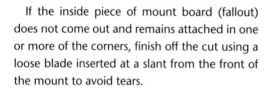

Using a bone paper folder to smooth down raised corners.

Using a blade to finish under-cuts by hand.

If the inside piece of mount board (fallout) does not come out and remains attached in one or more of the corners, finish off the cut using a loose blade inserted at a slant from the front of the mount to avoid tears.

Changing the gauge settings for cutting mounts with one or two different border measurements

For a weighted mount and other mount styles with mixed border measurements, both the border width gauge and the stop gauges will need to be adjusted before each cut.

CUTTING THE MOULDING

The moulding is cut so that the rebate lip overhangs the front of the mount or stretched canvas to hold the contents of the frame in from the front. A tray or inlay-style frame does not have a rebate lip so the contents, which will be a stretched canvas or a float-mounted board, are loaded from the front and fixed with screws through the tray into the back. A float-mounted board can be glued onto a wood plinth, which can be glued or screwed into the tray frame.

Allowing extra space for expansion or contraction

The moulding needs to be cut a little larger, about 1–2mm (a sixteenth of an inch) extra on each side, than the outside measurements of the mount. The extra measurement allows for expansion and contraction of materials in different temperatures. Glass in particular can break if the moulding is too tight around it.

Extra space is needed to accommodate the folds in the corners of a stretched canvas and more space is needed for a stretcher that has pegs in the back, which are tapped out to keep a canvas taut.

Using a mitre saw

Place the moulding in the saw with the rebate facing towards you. The back of the moulding must align against the fence at the back of the saw. There will be a clamp to secure the moulding while sawing. The saw blade is mounted on a bracket that can move to the left and right and be positioned to cut mitres for multiple sides frames. For a four-sided frame, 45-degree mitres are needed and a loud click at the extreme right and left positions of the

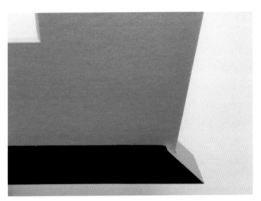

The rebate lip overhangs the edge of the mount board window.

Placing the moulding in the saw for the first cut; clamping the moulding and positioning the saw at the 45-degree angle.

saw indicate that the angle is true. To start the first side, a 45-degree mitre is cut on the end of the length of moulding. If you have a simple saw without a measuring tape it will be necessary to line the window mount up inside the mould-ing almost to the edge of the 45-degree mitre, between 1–2mm inside to allow room for expan-sion. Shade the edge of the rebate depth with pencil so that it is easier to judge the 1–2mm extra. Make a pencil mark along the rebate depth at the other end 1–2mm outside the length of the window mount and position the moulding in the saw so that the second pencil mark lines up with the sawing edge. If there is a measuring gauge fit-ted to the saw, it can be set against the 45-degree angle cut and left in place after sawing the mould-ing, so that the opposite side of the frame can be automatically cut to make another piece the same length without having to pencil mark the mould-ing against the window mount as before.

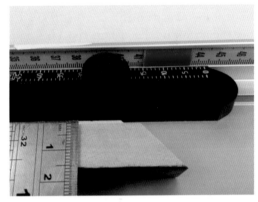

Setting the scale on an offset measuring gauge, using the width of the back of the moulding.

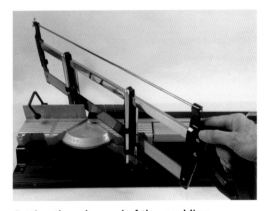

Cutting the other end of the moulding.

Using an offset measuring system

If the saw has a measuring system, there will be a scale to set the inside frame measurement. As there will be waste material from each cut amounting to twice the width of the frame excluding the rebate lip, this width measure-ment is lined up with the inside frame measure-ment on a special offset scale.

Using a mitre guillotine

Place the moulding into the mitre guillo-tine with the rebate facing away from you. The back of the moulding must be aligned against the fence at the front of the guillo-tine. After positioning the rebate support underneath the lip rebate, the right-hand end can then be trimmed in small stages to make a 45-degree mitre. Move the moulding through the machine to the right so that the new 45-degree mitre sits into the 45-degree mitre in the sliding measuring gauge. To set the required length, measure the width of the back of the moulding and use that figure on the sliding measuring gauge and line it up with the required length on the fixed scale. In this way, the scales are set to offset the waste material for a 45-degree mitre cut. The mould-ing is then cut to form two 45-degree mitres at once, making a series of small cuts by using a lever at the front of the machine, which moves the cutting platform forwards. The rebate pro-tectors need to be repositioned each time so that they remain under the rebate lip.

Using an offset scale on the mitre guillotine. The length to be cut is 41cm and it is placed against the top bar, which represents the width of the moulding minus the rebate lip (15mm in this example). A 1–2mm allowance for expansion has been added by moving the top measuring bar to the right.

Using a mitre trimmer

If the moulding is chipping, tearing, snagging or the fibres are being squashed when using a saw or guillotine, the blades may need sharp-ening, or the moulding may be particularly fragile. Cut the moulding slightly longer than is needed and then slice thin shavings off each end using a mitre trimmer. A mitre trimmer measuring gauge is available which screws on and will help to match the lengths for small-size

Placing the moulding in a mitre guillotine and positioning rebate protectors.

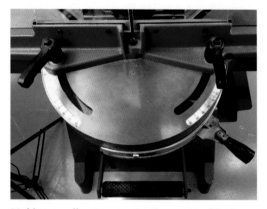

Making small cuts one at a time, repositioning the cutting platform forward by moving the lever to the right and readjusting the rebate protectors.

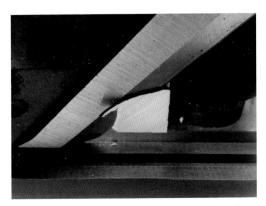

Positioning the 45-degree mitre cut in the mitre trimmer to shave off a sliver of wood.

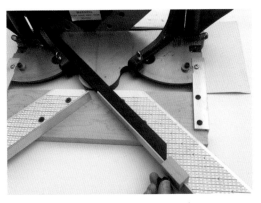

Matching two opposite lengths with a measuring gauge.

frames. To check that the lengths of the frame match without using a measuring gauge, place the two lengths back-to-back and run your finger across the two 45-degree mitre cuts to feel if they're different lengths. Slice off tiny slivers until they match.

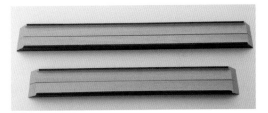

Matching lengths in two pairs.

Cutting frame-spacing fillet and slips

The fillet should be wide enough to fill the rebate lip, so that the edge of the artwork cannot be seen at the edges. Slips may be a little wider so that they show inside the frame to create an extra decorative effect. Cut the slip or fillet with a 45-degree mitre to fit inside the frame rebate.

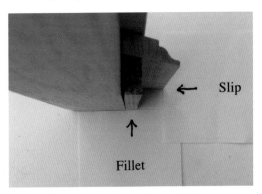

Fillets fit inside the rebate lip and slips protrude.

CUTTING SOLID METAL MOULDING

Solid metal moulding such as aluminium cannot be cut using framers' equipment. Order the size required from the manufacturer or supplier and they will cut it using specialized equipment. It will arrive with metal brackets and screws for fixing together.

FIXING AND JOINING

ATTACHING THE ARTWORK INTO THE WINDOW MOUNT

Tapes for fixing

White archival gummed tape

White archival gummed tape should be used to attach high-value artwork into the window mount. For extra strength use a white archival fabric-backed gummed tape.

After cutting the window mount, the pencil marks on the back can be erased.

White pH-neutral self-adhesive tape

White pH-neutral self-adhesive tape can be used to attach low-value artwork into the window mount. It is a high tack tape and if it needs to be removed, Zestit low odour solvent will dissolve the adhesive. Use a width of tape to suit the size of the mount and artwork and for extra strength, a fabric-backed self-adhesive tape.

Conserving the artwork

By sandwiching the artwork between the window mount and a backing barrier of conservation or museum quality, it is protected at the front and back from dampness and acidity. It is recommended to use mount board of the same thickness as the window mount as it will be a stable surface on which to attach the artwork (FATG).

Joining the window mount to the backing mount board

The window mount and backing mount are joined by a hinge of tape along the longest side regardless of the orientation of the artwork. If the orientation is landscape, then the taped hinge will be at the top. If the orientation is portrait, then the window mount is placed on the left so that the package opens like a book. The backing board is placed so that the back faces inside and the front is on the outside.

Taping the window mount to the backing mount board on the long sides.

Attaching the artwork inside the mount

Place the artwork inside and close the window mount on top. It is now possible to adjust the artwork so that it is straight, and the artist's signature is in view. A clean paperweight is then placed on top of the artwork and the window is lifted. A light pencil mark around each corner will help to reposition the artwork if it moves.

T-hinges

For most paper-based artwork, T-hinges can be made by tearing small pieces of white archival gummed tape that are 5mm longer than the width of the tape. Take care to keep the tear

Positioning the artwork inside.

Marking the corner positions with pencil.

Placing the wetted archival gum tape 5mm (¼ inch) under the artwork.

Placing a long piece of wetted archival gum tape on top of the previous pieces of gummed tape, without touching the artwork.

straight and even. Tear the same number of long pieces about three times the width of the tape. Tearing will make a chamfered edge, which is less likely to be seen under thin paper artwork. The small pieces of tape are fixed 5mm under the top of the artwork with the glue side facing up, after having been moistened. The long pieces are then moistened and placed glue-side down across the exposed part of the small pieces to form a T shape, while avoiding contact across the top of the artwork. The artwork is then hanging freely from the hinge and can remain flat.

White archival gummed tape has been threaded through reverse bevel slits top and bottom, leaving 5mm showing on the front.

OTHER METHODS OF MOUNTING ARTWORK

Float mounting

If the artwork is on deckle edge paper, or the paper is an odd shape, it can be float mounted on top of the mount board so that the edges are in view. Using the bevel cutter, cut reverse bevel slits in the mount board top and bottom. Feed about 3cm of gummed tape through the slit so that 5mm of the tape is hanging through on the front of the mount. Wet and attach at the back and wet the 5mm at the front to attach the artwork. For extra strength, attach extra tape across the back strips. A window mount can then be cut to allow extra space around the artwork, which helps to make an attractive feature of the uneven edges. The artwork should be no thicker than the window mount, or thicker mount board can be used.

Wetting the white archival gummed tape and positioning the artwork.

Shadow float mounting

Shadow float mounting is similar to float mounting except the artwork is mounted onto foam core to give it the effect of floating in space. Foam core thickness of 3, 5 or 10mm can be used and a moulding with an appropriate rebate depth. The foam core is cut 5mm smaller than the artwork. Although foam core is made of an inert material, conservation grade is available and also a fabric-faced version. Tear trips of white archival gummed tape long enough to wrap around the edge of the foam core with 5mm showing on the front and enough on the back to tape down. The art-

Fixing the tape on the back with self-adhesive pH-neutral tape.

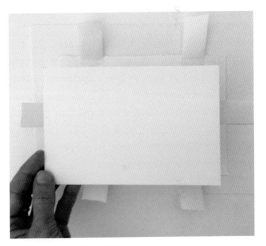

Placing 5mm (¼ inch) foam core.

Attaching white archival gummed tape 5mm (¼ inch) from the edge of the back of the artwork.

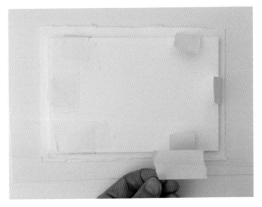

Taping in place with white self-adhesive pH-neutral tape.

Artwork floated and shadow floated seen from the front.

work goes on the front held in place with the 5mm tape ends. The tape is wrapped around to the back and held in place with a cross bar of the white gummed or self-adhesive tape. The foam core-mounted artwork can then be attached to a mount board. A fillet or spacer will be needed in the frame to prevent the artwork from touching the glass.

Fixing without direct contact with the artwork

These methods are for very fragile or valuable artwork that must not come in contact with either gummed tape or water because it could be devalued.

Artwork enclosed in clear polyester conservation quality film and attached to a mount board backing.

Encapsulation

It is enclosed in a clear polyester conservation-quality film and then taped by the edges of the film to attach it to the backing mount board. There are two brands available, one is called Mylar and one is called Melinex. Other methods include using a photo corner-style attachment with an L-shape overlap of clear film so that it doesn't show in the mount window, or thin strips of polyester film are available which strap across and are fed through a slit in the mount board and fastened on the back with tape. Archival see-through mounting strips can be used to hold art-work onto the backing mount by the edges. They have a narrow acid-free card edge that sticks to the backing mount with a self-adhesive backing, placed so it won't touch the artwork.

Held between two bevels

This holds the artwork in place without using tape, by holding the artwork at the edges between two bevelled window mounts. It is suitable for small artwork of thin card thickness.

JOINING THE MOULDING

Preparing the moulding for joining (sanding, clean sawn edges, clean rebate areas)

After sawing, the moulding may have some fuzzy fibres sticking out at the back where the saw has gone through the wood, which will pre-vent a good join. Place the frame pieces flat on a cutting board and slice them off with a craft knife. The rebate also may need to be carefully cleaned of any wood splinters, which may stop the glass from sitting evenly inside the frame. Additionally, the mitres can be coloured along the edges that will join together using a touch-up pen. This will help to conceal joins particu-larly for dark toned wood and black moulding

Using L-shaped polyester film corners.

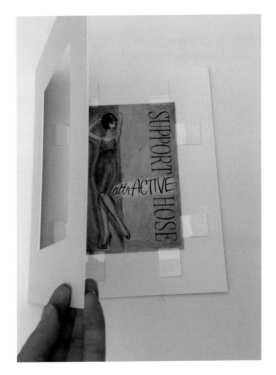

Using see-through mounting strips. Artwork by J.G. Bell, Carillon Press 1939 to 1969.

Selecting the right size V nail

Select the right size V nail for the moulding being joined. The V nail should be two thirds or three quarters of the height of the moulding so that it doesn't push through and damage the top face.

Cigarette card held between two bevelled window mounts.

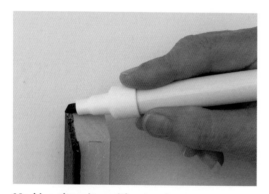

Marking the mitre with a touch-up pen.

Selecting the right size V nail taken from a ribbon of V nails showing the taped sharp ends that cut into the wood.

Gluing

PVA wood glue is spread sparingly over the 45-degree mitres. It is usually only necessary to apply the glue to one side of each corner. Wipe away any excess and avoid getting glue on the top face of the moulding if possible, particularly on a bare wood moulding that is to be dyed with a wood coloured stain, as the glue will repel the stain.

Hand-operated joiner

Corner clamp and strap clamp
The frame can be held together for pinning by either using a strap clamp, which holds the complete frame together, or by using a corner clamp, which holds together two corners at a time. If a corner clamp is being used, it will be necessary to adopt a system for making sure that each set of two frame sides is put together the same way.

Adjusting the bar height according to the height of the moulding
The hand lever of the joiner is adjusted up or down so that it will easily push a V nail down into the back of the moulding.

A hand-operated joiner has a magnetic post to hold a single V nail. The V nail must be placed

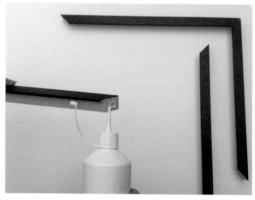

Applying wood glue to the mitres.

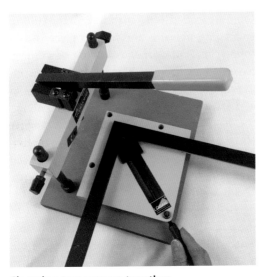

Clamping two corners together.

A V nail is attached to the magnetic post. Plunging the first V nail into the back of the two corners.

Using a strap clamp.

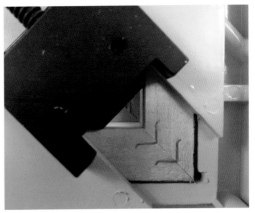

Two V nails inserted into the back of the frame.

with the sharp, cutting end at the bottom and the corner facing outwards. The lever is then pulled down and the V nail is plunged into the back of the moulding from the top down. According to the width of the moulding several V nails may be needed and they are placed first on the inside edge close to the rebate, then a little in from the outside edge, ensuring that the V nail does not pierce through the frame corner. Further V nails may be placed in between if needed. If the moulding is shaped in a way that it varies in height across its width, it may be necessary to use

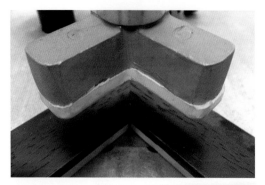

Mitred corners placed in a foot-operated underpinner.

V nails of different heights. Because the moulding is being pinned from the top down it may also be necessary to use a support under a shaped moulding, particularly a reverse bevel style, as trying to place V nails out towards the outside corners of the frame will cause the frame to tip over.

Foot-operated underpinner

The V nail is selected according to the height of the moulding and a ribbon is loaded into the underpinner. Some foot-operated underpinners use V nails that are supplied in a cassette and some are loaded into a channel with the cutting end facing upwards and held in place with a spring clip. Foot-operated underpinners usually have gauges to set one or more positions for inserting V nails. Place one side of the frame in and set the gauges for each position. As with the hand-operated underpinner, the plunger also is adjusted to suit the height of the moulding. In some parts of the frame two V nails can be put in, one after another, for extra strength. This is known as double banking. Extra care is needed to ensure the V nails are not too close to the outer corner, as they tend to veer outwards when double banked. Two pieces are joined to make a corner at a time so it is necessary to follow the same system as with the hand-operated joiner when placing the frame lengths in the underpinner, keeping the short sides to the left and the long sides to the right. The moulding is hand-held and pinned from the underneath by pressing a foot pedal. The third and fourth corners can be difficult to join, particularly if the frame is large and heavy as you will be joining together two L-shapes that tend to tip and roll. A support arm or bench the same height as the underpinner will solve this problem by keeping the frame straight and flat while corners three and four are pinned.

WHAT TO DO ABOUT GAPS

If there are any gaps in the corner joins, they can be filled with a wood filler made from PVA glue and sawdust. For bare wood moulding, it is then possible to apply a finish, anything from wax, dyes or paint. For a moulding that already has a finish, there are coloured waxes and gilt pastes to match. Ideally, it is better to solve the problem by using good quality, sharp sawing or mitre-cutting equipment, avoiding moulding that is warped, and checking that the moulding is lying flat when sawing or chopping.

Making wood filler with a mixture of glue and sawdust.

Fixing a stretched canvas into a frame

Apply brown, gummed tape to the back of the frame and fold any excess down inside the rebate. Once the tape is dry, the canvas can be fastened in the frame either with Z clips, turn buttons, or bendable metal plates. Turn buttons can only be used if the canvas fills the depth rebate so that it lies level. If the canvas is thinner or fatter than the depth rebate, Z clips or bendable plates have the flexibility to bend down into the rebate, or over a protruding canvas.

Using Z clips

One end of a Z clip is gently tapped into the inside of the rebate, two to four on each side before the canvas is placed inside. The canvas is then placed inside and positioned centrally. The Z clips are bent over and the other ends are tapped into the back of the canvas stretcher.

Using bendable plates

The canvas is placed into the frame and centrally positioned, then two to four plates are screwed onto the back of the frame on one edge and into the back of the canvas stretcher on the other edge. The plates can be bent to accommodate the width of the stretcher before fitting.

Fixing a stretched canvas or board into a tray-style frame

Because the whole image will be on view, it is essential that it is perfectly squared. Use a squaring angle to check, or measure the length between opposite corners. Even commercially prepared canvas boards can be out of true. Extra attention will be needed to see that the edges of the board or canvas are neat

HOW TO GET DENTS OUT OF BARE WOOD MOULDING

Moulding can dent easily if it is dropped, knocked or clamped too tightly, particularly obeche. Dents can be gently steamed out, because the wood fibres will plump up and straighten. Steaming works better on bare wood moulding, as gilt and paint finishes will inhibit the steam from entering the wood fibres, and can also be damaged.

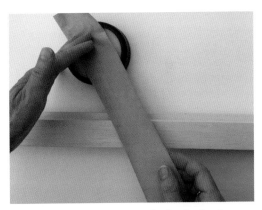

Applying gummed tape to the back of a frame.

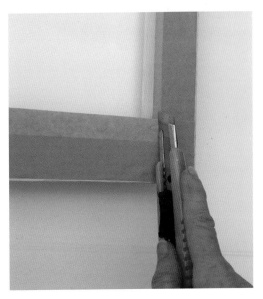

Slicing the gummed tape at the corners and folding the edges down into the rebate.

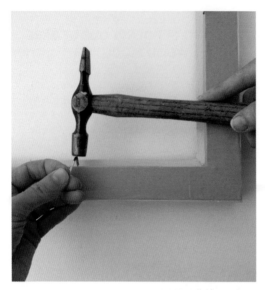

Hammering one end of a copper Z-clip into the back of the empty frame.

Hammering the other end of the copper Z-clip into the back of the canvas stretcher, which has been positioned in the frame.

Screwing eyelets into a tray-style frame for fixing a stretched canvas.

and tidy. To add to the general effect of the presentation, the artist can paint the edges of the board or canvas.

Stretched canvas

Fix several self-tapping eyelets on the lead edge of the tray frame on each side and screw them in parallel to the face of the bottom of the tray. Position the canvas centrally inside and screw a self-tapping screw through each eyelet into the back of the canvas stretcher bar. The back of the frame can then be neatened by applying brown gummed tape.

Board

A board may be made of plywood, or some other type of dense material. A painting or photograph on a board looks best if it is shadow-floated within a tray frame, particularly if the board is much thinner than the rebate depth. The board can be brought forward, or floated by resting it on a plinth made of wood fillet. The fillet is mitred, pinned and glued to make a frame about 5mm smaller than the board around the

Placing a canvas in from the front.

Screwing self-tapping screws through the eyelets into the back of the canvas.

edges. The fillet frame can then be glued onto the inside of the tray frame and the board glued and positioned into the frame. When the glue has dried, the back of the frame can be neatened by applying brown gummed tape.

Board or panel and wooden plinth ready to be glued into a tray frame. Fibre Paste Flowers, acrylic painting by Elaine Scott.

BACKING BOARD, GLASS AND ASSEMBLY

CUTTING BACKING BOARD

The final backing board, which gives firm support from behind, can be cut with a craft knife to the same size as the external window mount size. It must have a little room to move inside the frame, for possible expansion. Keep a small offcut for use as a landing mat when using a glass cutter.

Measuring the backing board.

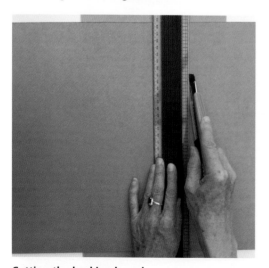

Cutting the backing board.

GLASS

When it's cold in your work area, cutting glass can be a problem. It may shatter, or refuse to snap entirely. Glass needs to be a minimum temperature of 10 degrees Celsius (50 degrees Fahrenheit) to snap smoothly.

Handling glass

When handling glass, always hold it with two hands at the top to prevent it from twisting. Glass will break easily, even with a slight twist. It can also chip on the edges if placed on a hard floor or ground. A soft mat or carpet in the storage area will help protect the edges. Rubber glass-handling gloves allow safe handling when moving glass, and rubber suckers are needed for very large sheets that span wider than arm's length. For personal safety, wear non-slip, closed shoes when carrying large sheets of glass. Sweep or vacuum the workbench free of glass shards before laying the glass down, as they can scratch the surface. Lay glass down onto the workbench evenly with two hands placed along the top edge.

Measuring, scoring and snapping glass

Glass can either be measured by placing it for a loose fit on top of the frame, with the back of the frame facing up or, if the frame has a deep rebate and placing on top will risk breakage, measure with a ruler or use a T square. Measure the longest side of the mount first and mark the glass top and bottom using a glass marker pen.

Place a small offcut of backing board against the edge where the glass cutter will arrive as a landing pad; if it is the same thickness as the glass it will lessen the chance of it chipping on the edge as the score is ended. Lubricating the glass cutter before use will ensure a smooth score, and extend the life of the glass cutter head. Line up the middle of the cutting head with the top mark, then the bottom mark against a non-slip ruler or T square. The glass cutter must be held firmly in a vertical position and starting from the far side, in contact with the ruler, draw the glass cutter towards yourself with firm, even pressure. There is a distinctive scratch sound and the scratch line should be continuous across the glass. If the line is not continuous, or too faint, the glass may not snap evenly. Re-scoring in the same groove will damage the glass cutter, so it is recommended to turn over and score it on the other side instead. After scoring, the glass can be snapped in different ways. Wear eye protection just in case any glass particles fly upwards and glass-handling gloves to protect the hands from splinters. One way of snapping glass is to hold the glass between forefingers and thumbs either side of the score and open outwards. Another way is to tap along the score line with the special glass-snapping ball featured on the end of some glass cutters. Yet another way is to place a ruler under the glass, close to the score line, and apply downward pressure to the unsupported piece of glass.

When cutting large sheets of glass, score and gently pull it to the edge of the workbench and line the score up so that the weight of the glass will naturally allow it to snap and drop into your hands.

Measuring and marking the glass with a glass-marking pen.

Lining the glass-cutting wheel with the mark.

Scoring the glass with the glass-cutter held upright.

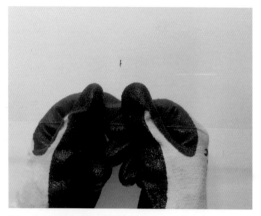

Wearing glass-handling gloves and eye goggles, hold the glass with the thumbs and forefingers and open outwards from the score line.

The glass breaks along the score line.

Spray glass cleaner onto lint-free cloth.

Cleaning the glass.

Cleaning glass

Glass can be cleaned with a lint-free cloth dampened with pH-neutral glass cleaner, or deionized water. Many commercial glass cleaners are too alkaline and contain chemicals that could damage artwork.

Scoring and snapping speciality glass

Some speciality glass has a coating on both surfaces, in which case either side can be scored. Speciality glass with a soft acrylic coating on one side must be scored on the non-coated surface. The glass is supplied and labelled showing the coated side.

Scoring and snapping acrylic glazing

Although it is easier to handle than glass, acrylic glazing can craze or crack if it is dropped. It has a protective coat of plastic sheeting on both sides, which should be left in place while scoring. Measure the glazing using the same method as for glass and use a special tool designed for scoring acrylic. It may be necessary to make several passes with the scoring tool, depending on the thickness of the acrylic. It can be snapped by bending open along the score, or bending on the edge of a workbench. Remove the plastic sheeting both sides and assemble the frame straight away as static electricity will attract dust onto the glazing.

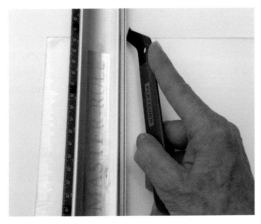

Scoring acrylic glass.

Snapping acrylic glass.

ASSEMBLY

Stack the components of the frame from the backing board up to the frame, checking for dust particles on each level, using a soft brush to sweep clean, a mini dust extractor or anti-static roller. Dust that adheres to a fabric item or fabric-faced mount board can be removed with a piece of light tack masking or picture tape.

EASY METHOD FOR REMOVING DUST

Roll a piece of Scotch 811 removable tape around a finger with the sticky side facing out, and use to remove fine dust on the window mount. Masking tape can be used in the same way to remove dust from glass and fabric art. Test the tape to see how tacky it is first and reduce tackiness if necessary by dabbing it on some fabric.

Tabs and tab guns

Temporary flexi tabs can be used, a couple fired into each corner of the depth rebate for checking that all dust is out. When the glass is pressed against the mount it may show dust

Firing tabs into the back of the frame.

that could not be seen before fixing. This part of the framing project is best left for daylight hours. The flexi tab will bend to allow you to open and close the frame as many times as necessary to remove all dust. Glass tends to magnify dust and imperfections when it is pressed against the mount board. Once all the dust has gone, permanent rigid tabs are fired into the depth rebate at regular intervals. To prevent the sides of the frame from bowing out, rest the side that is being pinned against a support bar.

Tape

Two types of tape can be used to seal the frame at the back, either self-adhesive brown picture tape, or brown gummed tape. A good quality self-adhesive tape is acceptable and fast to use. Gummed tape needs to be wetted evenly so it helps to use a gummed tape dispenser. Select a tape that is wide enough to fit across the width of the frame and cover the tabs in the back of the frame. If there is still some rebate depth left at the back of the frame, slice the tape at the corners and fold down neatly onto the backing board.

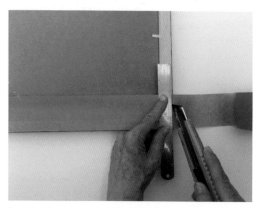

Positioning brown self-adhesive picture tape on the back of the frame and cutting with a craft knife.

Slicing the ends to fold the tape down into the remaining rebate.

Folding the tape neatly into the rebate.

Placing a fillet made of wood and mount board inside a frame.

From left: Window mount with slip, then a frame slip, then glass and frame.

Assembling a glazed frame without a window mount

After cleaning the glass, place it in the frame followed by either a decorative slip or fillet spacer, which may be made of wood or plastic. Clear plastic fillets known as EconoSpace have a self-adhesive edge, which sticks to the back of the glass. They are available in several sizes and are very quick and convenient to use. Wood fillets will need a few spots of glue to keep them in place. The wood fillet will either have a paper covering or it will need tape placed along the edge where it comes into contact with the artwork. This operates as a barrier to stop the resin coming from the wood. Then artwork can be placed inside the frame supported by mount board behind and finally, the backing board, tabs and tape.

Attaching fixings, cord or wire and bumpers

Fixings
D-rings and self-tapping screws are a popular way of attaching cord to the back of the frame. They have the advantage of laying flat against the back of the frame, which reduces the danger of damage to other picture frames during transport and storage. Position the fixings by measuring a third down from the top of the frame and use a bradawl to make small pilot holes for screwing the D-rings into place.

Cord
Select nylon cord appropriate to the size and weight of the frame and cut a length twice the width of the frame with extra to spare. The cord should be angled up to a maximum of 120 degrees to ensure even weight distribution. The length needs to be twice the width of the picture frame to create a loop, which goes through

Making small pilot holes with a bradawl a third of the frame height from the top.

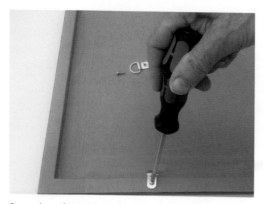

Screwing the D-rings into position with self-tapping screws.

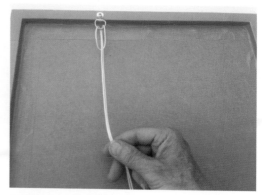

Making a cow hitch with a double length of cord.

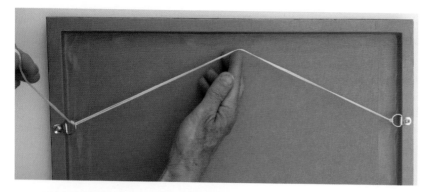

Checking the angle of the cord and tying the other end with half hitch knots.

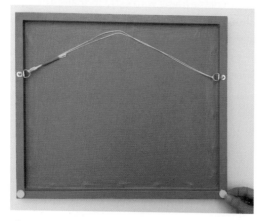

The end of the cord has been taped. Attaching bumpers.

one of the D-rings, then loops through itself to create a cow hitch. The two ends of the cord are then to be threaded through the opposite D-ring, and round and through again, finishing with two half hitches and with the ends bound off with tape.

Wire

Feed the end of the wire through the D-ring from the inside of the frame, around and back under the wire and through the D-ring for a second time, to make a slip knot. Twist the remaining loose wire around itself four or five times and snip off the end with pliers. Cut the wire the width of the frame arched up so that the wire is at an angle no greater than 120 degrees with about an extra 10cm (4 inches) for knotting.

Bumpers

Self-adhesive bumpers made of felt or cork are placed at the back of the frame in the bottom corners to keep the frame away from the wall. The effect is an increase of air circulation between the picture and the wall, for preventing dampness. The corners of the frame won't mark the wall and the frame is more likely to hang straight.

Fixings for framing a mirror or a notice board

Mirror

For a very heavy mirror, use a strap fitting and for a very light mirror, double D-rings may be sufficient. Use a chain for a very heavy mirror, or heavy-duty cord. Alternatively, the mirror can be attached to the wall using mirror plates or sliding hooks, which are fixed at the back of the frame and cannot be seen from the front.

Notice board

A notice board needs to be evenly flat and fixed against the wall so that it doesn't move when notices are pinned. Mirror plates can be fixed at the sides and screwed into the wall. Hooks which work as a pair and slide into each other can be screwed onto the back of the frame and the wall, then slotted into each other and the effect is invisible fastening.

Fixings for a stretched canvas

Select fixings according to the weight and size of the frame from single D-rings or double D-rings to strap rings. The fittings should be attached to the back of the frame, one third down from the top. Select the cord, cut and attach in the same way as described in the section 'Attaching fixings, cord or wire and bumpers' above.

Finished picture frame.

> **FINALLY**
>
> If there are any rough edges on the outside corners of the frame, sand them off using a fine sanding block, taking care not to round off corners and then apply a cream filler to match. Check the joins for any gaps and fill with the wood filler and finish with the cream filler.

Fixings for a stand-up photograph frame

Backing boards with a ready-made stand incorporated, called strut backs, are available for standard-sized photograph frames or a metal stand that slots onto the edge of the backing board before it is put into the frame. Because the back of the photograph frame will at times be in view, the strut back has a black backing paper. Black tape is available as an alternative to brown picture tape for sealing the edges. If frequent access is needed to change the photograph, the depth rebate can be filled with thicker board so that the contents are level. Turn keys are then fitted to the back of the frame.

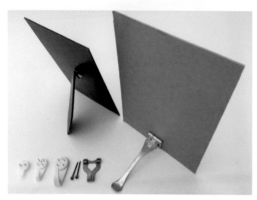

Hard wall Toly hooks in three sizes; metal picture hook; metal strut and card strut back.

Pencil portraits displayed on decorative metal easels. Linnette and Rebecca (circa 1973) by Gareth Bell.

TRANSPORTING A FRAME

Now that your first frame is completed, it is ready to hang or transport. Always carry it by the cord with one hand, and support with the other, or with two hands on either side of the frame. Lifting with one hand or holding at the top can cause strain on the glass and moulding.

DISPLAYING

Hanging

When hanging the picture, avoid areas of strong sunlight to prevent fading, and hanging over radiators because of heat rising. Pictures can deteriorate faster in areas of high humidity such as kitchens and bathrooms.

Picture hooks

If the wall is very hard, plastic Toly hooks will be easier to use. They are available in three sizes and are simply placed against the wall while four small pins in the Toly hook are hammered. There is a hole in the centre for hammering an extra nail. For all other walls use metal picture hooks and picture hook nails. Sometimes two picture hooks may be needed to keep a picture straight.

Display easels

Easels allow the frame to be displayed tilted back slightly and resting on top of a piece of furniture, or on the floor. They are available in wood or metal and can be a simple design, or ornate.

Ledges for mirrors or other pictures

For a very heavy mirror, a ledge or shelf in addition to wall fixings can give extra support and also be an extra decorative feature.

VARIATIONS ON MOUNT CUTTING

DOUBLE MOUNT

Plan two mount boards of different colours or one colour. They can be laid out next to the edge of the artwork and a ruler used to measure the chosen width of the top and bottom mount. Make a note of the colour and mount width, for example top white 5cm (2 inches), bottom black 6cm (2¼ inches). Measure and cut three boards using the window size and twice the border width of the bottom mount, for example window size and 6cm (2¼ inches) twice. Cut the bottom mount board a little smaller, 5mm (¼ inch) all round. The top mount is marked up with the planned border width and cut using a slip mat underneath. Keep the fallout in place and turn the whole piece face down on the worktop. The fallout remains in the centre as temporary support material. Masking tape rolled into loops is attached to the fallout, while permanent strips of double-sided masking tape are attached to the back of the window mount itself, close to the inside edge. Then place the bottom mount board with the front side facing down squarely on top of the taped area. Because it is a little smaller, a little of the back of the top mount will be in view on all sides. Press the two mounts together and mark up the border for the bottom mount on the back, which will come further inside the top mount border lines. The artwork can be placed over the pencil marks to check the fit. Cut the bottom mount without the slip mat in place. The two fallouts should fall out together, but if they don't, gently peel

A double mount.

Planning and recording the widths of the top and bottom mount windows.

off the top one and use a blade to finish the corners of the bottom mount. You will achieve a perfectly lined up double mount, which is nearly impossible if each is cut separately and attached afterwards. Attach the artwork using the third mount board as described in Chapter 4.

USING BLACK CORE MOUNT BOARD

When using black core mount board take care not to place it against a black or other dark-coloured mount board or artwork, because the black bevel effect will be lost.

Variations

The width of the bottom mount can be varied; it is generally much narrower than the top mount, and it is not recommended to make it the same width because the resulting stripy effect may be too dominant. Another effect is to make the top mount very narrow, rather like a mount board slip.

FAUX DOUBLE MOUNT

Often known as an inlay, this is a way of making the effect of a double mount while retaining the thickness of a single mount. It is useful if non-reflective glass is going to be used, where a double mount may create too much distance between the image and the glass, to cause a slightly blurred effect. It can also be helpful if the moulding depth rebate is too shallow to accommodate a regular double mount.

Plan the border widths for the outside and inside or inlay mount. The overall mount board size is calculated by adding the required border width and the thin width of visible inlay to the window size. Stick the smaller board face down onto the back of the larger board with a strip of double-sided tape, placed in the centre. Mark the outside border width on the back of the boards. Cut the border on the back mount, taking care not to cut too deeply into the front mount. There is no need to use a slip mat because of the double thickness. Remove the outer border from the back mount and discard, then draw light pencil lines across each side, across the centre mount card and the exposed back of the front

Sticking the bottom mount board onto the back of the top mount board using double-sided tape around the mount and double-sided tape on the fallout, which is kept in place as a support. The bottom mount is slightly smaller.

The bottom mount borders are marked. Their lines come inside the top mount lines and now checking for fit before cutting.

Planning and recording the widths of the outside mount and inlay.

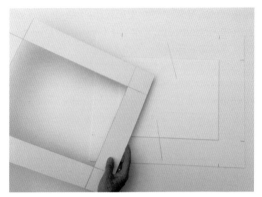

Removing the outside border of the bottom mount and discarding. Marking registration lines before removing the small inside fallout.

After re-marking the border in the same place and cutting, the fallouts have been swapped, aligning the registration marks and taped in using white self-adhesive pH-neutral tape.

Completed faux double or inlay mount.

card so that the card can be repositioned in the same place. Peel the back card off and cut the same width border as before with the slip mat in the mount cutter.

After removing the fallout, replace it with the small back card, aligning the pencil marks for a perfect fit, tape together with white self-adhesive pH-neutral tape. Finally, having planned the total width of the window mount, mark up and cut with the slip mat in place.

BACKING PAPER

Replace the backing paper on double-sided tape so that it doesn't prevent the mount cutter from moving during the cut.

Inlay border

An inlay border or strip can be created by laying the mount face down after having taped the second fallout inside, place the first fallout on top and draw a border for the other side of the strip. Draw the border across the fallout and the mount underneath. Cut the fallout and remove the outside border. Draw pencil registration lines and peel the fallout off. Mark the bottom mount with the same border width, cover the double-sided tape and cut the border. Swap the fallouts, tape in and cut the final window to fit the artwork.

Planning and recording measurements for an inlay border mount.

The window is then cut to fit the artwork.

REVERSE BEVEL

A reverse bevel is useful if a decorative fillet is used against the inside of the window mount, as a regular bevel will show a white line. When mounting dusty artwork such as soft pastels and charcoal drawings, the dust will be trapped behind the bevel out of sight. Sometimes a clean edge without a bevel is preferred, especially when making a double mount with two very bold colours. The border width is set and marked as usual but with basic mount cutters, the cutting ruler must be on the other side of the line and covering the fallout. Some more professional mount cutters have a reverse bevel gauge, so that the required border width is set and the mount cutter is moved across and rests against the gauge to enable cutting on the other side of the mount window.

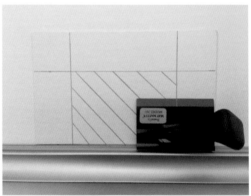

Mount cutter in position for a regular bevel cut.

Mount cutter in position for a reverse bevel cut.

Double mounts cut as regular and reverse bevels.

MULTIPLE WINDOW MOUNT

Two or more pieces of artwork are arranged together on one mount, each with their individual window. The images could be about an event or a topic and a title or date box may be included. The colour of the mount board is selected to complement all the images, which should be related. Try different colours by placing the images as a group on top and see how each colour has a general impact. If a mount colour is chosen that appears in any of the images,

the eye will be drawn more to that part of the image. The outside border should be wider than the mount spaces between the images to make them look united as a whole. Once an arrangement has been decided, draw a simple plan and write down each horizontal and vertical measurement including the outside border, the window size for each image, the gaps in between and the outside border on the other side. Cut the board to the measurements. Draw the outside border width then, using a sharp pencil, mark the position of each window for each image. If the arrangement is asymmetrical, it is helpful to turn all the images upside down on the worktop to be

Planning the arrangement and measuring horizontally and vertically.

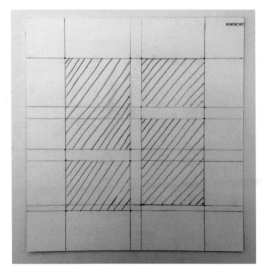

Marking the board out on the back and reversing the images so that they appear on the correct side.

Checking the images for fit before cutting.

able to see them as they need to be drawn on the back of the mount board. Some individual images may extend beyond or are smaller than others, so extra lines will need to be drawn extended to the edge of the mount board to ensure that edges are lined up in the mount cutter accurately. Mark the corners of each window with a highlighter and draw slash marks across the back of each fallout,

then cut all the outside borders of the windows. Cut the internal borders taking care to turn the mount board so that it is on the correct side of the mount cutter rail with the slashed fallouts in view, to avoid cutting a reverse bevel.

Multiple double mount

To make a multiple double mount, select two mount board colours and decide the visible width of the bottom mount. Measure the height and width of each image and add on an extra 10mm (½ inch) on each measurement if you require 5mm (¼ inch) of the bottom mount to show, or 20mm (1 inch) for 10mm (½ inch) to show. Using the top mount measurements across and down the arrangement, add them up and cut the top board. Using the top mount measurements, mark out each window taking care to extend all the lines to the edges of the mount board and cut out the windows as before, retaining the fallouts as support material, place the mount face down on the worktop. Cut the bottom mount board

Finished multiple image mount.

The lines have been marked on the back of the bottom mount inside the top mount lines. The images have been placed to check for fit.

slightly smaller, about 5mm (¼ inch) all round and using double-sided tape around each window and masking tape rolled into loops in the centre of each fallout, place the bottom mount face down on top and press firmly. Reset the border width on the mount cutter for the bottom mount, draw the outside border and then use the extension lines visible at the edges of the top mount as a guide to draw the windows on the bottom mount to the planned width. The new lines will be 5mm (¼ inch) or 10mm (½ inch) inwards on each image from the previous lines. Check that each image fits, then start by cutting the outside borders. Cut the rest of the borders taking care to cut on the correct side of the cutting rail. The centres should all fall out easily, but if they don't, gently peel off the top mount fallouts and slice the corners of any that are attached.

Leaf print collection in a double mount. Artwork by the author.

OFFSET CORNER MOUNT

An offset corner mount is just a regular mount with corners overhanging the image. Add the window size and twice the border measurement as usual, then cut the mount board and mark the border with pencil. The artwork can be tested to fit inside these lines but now a second set of lines is drawn inside. The distance between these two sets of lines will determine the size of the overhanging corner. Highlight the corners to be cut with a colour and plan to cut the outside lines first, using the inside lines to start and stop the cut. Cut the inside lines using the outside lines to start and stop the cut. If you plan to make a double mount, keep all the fallout in one piece by only cutting at each end on the inside cut, to leave the middle attached.

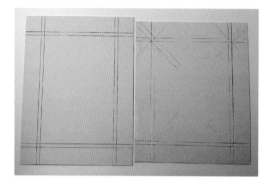

The lines for offset and angle mounts are marked on the back of the mount board. The artwork is laid on top to check for fit.

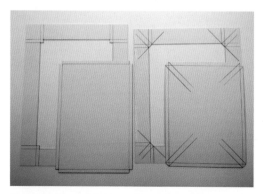

The mounts and fallouts from the offset corner and angle cut.

Double mount combinations

For a double mount, keep the fallout in place and place another board, cut slightly smaller, face down on the back. Attach with double-sided tape around the edges and rolls of masking tape on the fallout as for a double mount. The offset corner can be repeated, or a simple straight cut looks very attractive in combination with the offset corner.

ANGLE-CUT MOUNT

An angle-cut mount is a regular mount with an angle overhanging the image. Prepare the mount board in the same way as for the offset corner mount and place the artwork over the lines to check that it fits. Draw a second set of lines inside and long diagonal lines across each corner for lining up to the edge of the mount cutter. Draw long start and stop lines that will be visible on the other side of the mount-cutter head, by placing a ruler along each diagonal line with a set square against it to make a true 90-degree angle. Mark the cutting areas with a highlighter pen and cut the borders starting and stopping at the inside line. Place the mount in the mount cutter at an angle and holding it steady, cut the angles on each corner.

Double mount combinations

To make a double angle mount, or combine with a straight cut, measure and cut the top mount. Fix the bottom mount on the back. Then measure in from the sides and angles to the desired width, for example 5mm (¼ inch) or 10mm (½ inch).

From the left: Offset corner decoration and angle cut mounts. *Ladies* artwork by Alexandra Zillweger.

From the left: Offset corner and angles combined with inner straight cuts. *Ladies* artwork by Alexandra Zillweger.

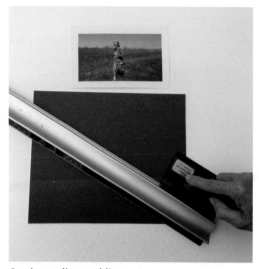

Cutting a diagonal line.

Diagonal lines cut, ready to be taped together on the back.

STRIPES

Draw an angled or horizontal line on the back of a piece of mount board and cut using the mount cutter. Cut a strip of mount board in a contrasting colour using a reverse bevel cut on one edge and a regular bevel cut on the other edge. Tape the strip in between the two pieces of mount board using white self-adhesive pH-neutral tape. Trim, mark and cut out the window.

Diagonal strip mount and horizontal stripes. From left: Linda Dowell (photo: Graeme Stringer); Karen Rees in *Chasing the Ferries* (photo: Jonathan Tribbeck).

V GROOVE

A V groove is a decorative effect placed a little distance from the inside edge of the window mount and created with two bevel cuts facing each other to form a V shape. Add the window size and two border widths, and cut the board. Draw the border for the window size on the back and the position for the V groove a little further out, such as 10mm (½ inch). Draw a pencil registration mark across the lines and then cut along the V groove line. Turn the fallout up the right way and trim off the bevel edge all the way round discarding the thin strips of mount board each time so they don't get caught in the mount cutter. Hold the mount cutter down firmly while cutting so the mount board doesn't slip. A strip of mount board placed against the edge when cutting gives the mount-cutter head a flat surface at the same height as the mount board being cut. Some mount cutters have a V groove stop which helps to cut just the right amount of bevel off. Replace the fallout back into the window, lining up the registration marks and tape across the cut using white archival gummed or white self-adhesive tape according to the value of the artwork. You should end up with an attractive white core V shape. Place back in the mount cutter and cut the window out as usual.

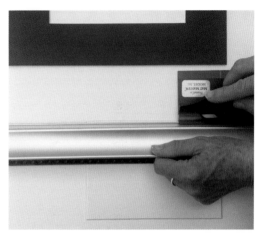

Trimming the reverse bevel edge off the fallout with a piece of mount board butted up against the edge to support the cutter.

A V groove decoration on a mount. Artwork by the author.

HOW TO PREPARE AND FRAME FABRIC ART

PREPARING THE FABRIC ART

Handling fabric artwork

With clean, dry hands, lay the fabric on a clean, dry surface to examine and prepare. It is not recommended to cut any loose threads even if they are at the back, or trim the fabric. Cleaning, washing and straightening fabric is best left to the maker, or a conservator if it is an old, valuable piece.

Padding fabric art with polyester wadding.

Conservation

Vegetable fibres such as cotton, rayon and viscose can be damaged in time if they are in contact with an acidic surface. Animal protein materials such as silk and wool should not be in contact with buffered mount board as they can be harmed by an alkaline environment, so unbuffered 100 per cent cotton rag should be used.

Padding and stretching the fabric

There may be imperfections in fabric art such as loose or broken threads, knots, beads or tight stitches causing the material to pucker. The effect can be reduced by placing some padding behind, such as polyester felt or wadding bought from a haberdashery store.

Lacing
The lacing method is suitable for fabric art based on a strong support with enough fabric to go round the back of a board, for example cross stitch, embroidery, appliqué or needlepoint. Depending on the weight and size of the fabric, conservation or museum-grade mount board, or foam core in thickness of 3 (⅛ inch), 5 (¼ inch) or 10mm (½ inch) can be used. Cut a perfect straight-edged piece of board with at least an extra 4mm (¼ inch) larger than the viewable area of the fabric art to allow for the overlap of

Positioning over a board cut larger than the window size.

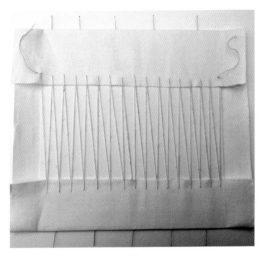

Lacing along the long sides.

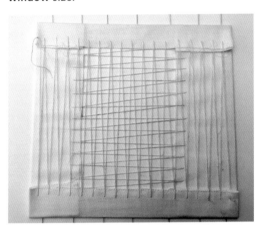

Lacing along the short sides.

Finished with a double mount. Stitched cross stitch, Fishing Boats design by John Clayton reproduced by permission of Heritage Crafts Ltd, Rugeley, UK.

a window mount. Lay the fabric on top of the board and using a ruler, check that the image is evenly placed. Stainless steel pins can then be placed into the edges, to pin the fabric to the board starting in the centre of each side and pinning out to the edges. Once pinned, the fabric is turned over and the excess fabric folded over. Starting with the longest edges, lace from side to side using a thread of similar weight to fabric. Check the positioning from the front and adjust if necessary, then repeat the lacing with the short sides.

Wooden stretcher bars

A simple way of presenting a silk or batik would be to stretch it over a wooden stretcher. Pre-cut stretcher bars can be used, which slot together and can be pegged out if a canvas becomes slack, or a stretcher bar moulding, which is cut and mitred. Stretcher bars are generally made of pine, so they will need sealing with an undercoat of paint to prevent the sap from leaching into the fabric. The fabric can then be hung as it is,

The artwork is stretched over the top of the stretched support fabric.

Leaving unframed. Silk fabric print from a design by the author.

Framed in a tray-style frame.

with the image around the side, known as a gallery wrap, or it can be framed in a tray frame. A piece of polyester canvas the same size as the fabric art will be needed to give extra strength to delicate material. Staple the support canvas to the frame, first using staples in the centre of each side and placing additional staples out towards the corners, firmly stretching the canvas in the process, stop at about 10cms (4 inches) from the corners giving working space for folding the corners. Fold the corners to lay flat and staple at the back, avoiding stapling across corners if using a stretchable

stretcher as explained in Chapter 2. Lay the silk or other thin fabric on top and repeat the process. The stretched fabric can be left unframed, or framed in a tray frame. Fitting in a tray frame is described in Chapter 4.

Tight fit or Newberry method

A tight fit allows a fine, delicate fabric such as silk to be pinched between an outer border and the inside support of mount board or foam core with or without additional need for stitches or pins. There needs to be sufficient fabric around the edges of the planned window size to fold behind the support. Add the window size to twice the border width for the height and width of the fabric art and cut a piece of foam core, or thick conservation mount board. Mark a border in pencil 4 to 5mm (¼ inch) narrower than your final mount border and using a ruler and craft knife, make a straight cut along each side. A little over-cut in each corner is all right as it will allow the centre to be removed cleanly and it won't be seen later. The fabric is centred and lined up on the piece of mount board or foam core from the centre and the outside border is pressed on top to gently stretch and grip the fabric. This method is named after Stoney

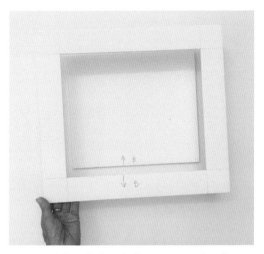

Cut a straight window in foam core and make registration marks to replace in the same position.

Squaring the fabric art over the fallout and replacing the window on top to stretch the material flat.

Double mount is cut smaller than the foam core window.

Newberry, who developed this way of creating a flat surface for a mount to lay on top. When using this method for thicker fabrics, trim off some of the foam core border on the inside so that it can fit easily. Stretch the fabric over the centre piece and either pin on the edges, or lace at the back.

Sew on fabric support or extension and pinning

A fabric support chosen to complement the fabric art is a useful method for supporting a fragile and possibly irregular-shaped piece of fabric art. The support fabric can be pinned to a piece of foam core around the edges and then the fabric art can be positioned. Use a few small invisible stitches through the fabric art and fasten on the back of the foam core without cutting through any of the threads of

Delicate irregular-shaped silk attached to a silk support and pinned over foam core. Fabric art by Coral Slade.

After folding and arranging, a pattern for the insert is traced on tissue paper.

A support board for the body and each sleeve is cut from museum-quality mount board.

the fabric art. For extra security, tape over the stitches on the back of the foam core using pH-neutral white adhesive tape.

If there is just insufficient fabric around the edge of a straight-sided piece to lace or pin, a strip of fabric of the same kind can be sewn on the edge, which will be concealed by a window mount.

Preparing a T-shirt or other item of clothing

The clothing may be folded, for example the sleeves of a shirt, but if left in full view will make the overall display area large. Once the arrangement has been decided, the unfolded areas will need a support inside to gently stretch creases out and stop them from flopping. Cut a shaped support from conservation- or museum-quality mount board, smoothing off any sharp corners that could snag or tear fabric or yarn and insert the mount board inside the garment. Fold and straighten into position ready to attach to the front of a mount board, which has been cut to the planned glass size.

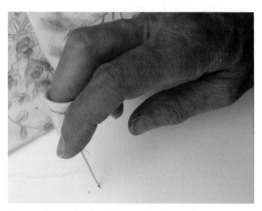

The jacket is laid out on a backing of museum-quality mount board and holes are made in pairs so that thread can be looped through and tied at the back of the mount board.

Fixing the jacket and support board at the neck and shoulders with looped stitches.

Shadow float-mounted tapestry in a tray-style frame. Fabric art *Urban Reflections* designed and made by Matty Smith.

Tying off the threads at the back of the mount board and securing with white pH-neutral self-adhesive tape.

Making pairs of needle-size holes in museum-quality mount board, being careful not to pierce the threads of the crotchet collar.

Making small invisible loops of thread to tie off at the back and tape over.

Tying the threads at the back of the board.

Float mount and shadow float mount methods for attaching the fabric

These methods may be useful if the fabric has an attractive edge such as a fringe that needs to be left in view. The float method is suitable for clothing, such as signed football or rugby T-shirts, or other items of fabric-based memorabilia. A complementary piece of mount board is chosen and the fabric is laid, arranged and attached using discrete stitches that go through the fabric and tie at the back of the mount board. A bradawl or sharp needle can be used to make small holes in the mount board in strategic positions before sewing. After sewing,

using white pH-neutral adhesive tape, tape over the stitches on the back of the mount board for added security. The fabric can be given the impression of floating above the mount board by adding a piece of foam core between the fabric and the mount board. Cut the foam core 5mm (¼ inch) smaller all around than the fabric art. Position it on top of the mount board with some double-sided tape in each corner, then attach the fabric with discrete stitches through all thicknesses to the back of the mount board and tape over the stitches as before. The shadow float method will work best on fabric that is not too floppy, so that the edges remain straight.

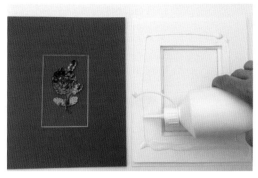

After attaching the foam core spacer onto the back of the window mount with double-sided tape, apply glue on the back.

The mount can be positioned easily onto the bottom mount window to create extra depth.

PLANNING THE MOUNT OR SPACER

The mount plays an important role in keeping the fabric away from the glass to prevent moisture being transferred to the fabric, flattening of stitch work or other damage that could be caused by glass pressing on fabric, for example broken beads. Choose a mount design with the appropriate amount of depth to protect the fabric art, with a minimum thickness created by a double mount or a single mount of 3,500 microns' thickness. If the fabric art is very large, or a mount is not wanted, then a fillet or slip can be used to separate the fabric from the glass. Some fabric work such as a rug or tapestry may not need glazing.

Double mount

Select two colours that complement the fabric art and plan the widths for the borders. Follow the process described in Chapter 6. Once the mount is cut, it is ready to be placed on top of the fabric prepared using the lacing, pinned or Newberry methods.

Double mount with foam core spacer

Prepare a double mount using two boards the same size and a small amount of double-sided tape to hold them together while cutting the bottom mount. Carefully peel the mounts apart and attach strips of foam core about 10mm (½ inch) narrower than the top mount, so it cannot be seen from the side. Sandwich the two mounts together again using double-sided tape on one side and some PVA glue on the other side to allow time for lining up the edges of the two mounts.

Circle and oval mounts

Oval and circle mounts look good on single centralized designs that don't cover the whole of the support fabric. They can also help to divert the eye from the warp and weft of fabric that is not quite square. Double mounts can be cut separately and taped together with the addition of a foam core oval or circle border as a spacer in between, if required.

Double oval and circle mounts look good on centralised designs. Cross stitch Woodpecker and Robin designed and stitched by Elaine Barr.

Deep bevel mount made with wrapped foam core

Strips of wrapped, bevel-edge foam core are attached onto the back of a window mount to achieve a deep decorative bevel. Four strips of foam core 5mm (¼ inch) or 10mm (½ inch) thick,

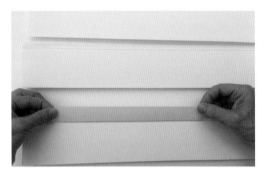

Applying the decorative tape to the foam core strips.

The foam core strips are bound on the edges with decorative tape.

the width of the window border, are cut using a special foam core cutter with a blade angled to make a bevel. The ruler of the mount cutter can be used to run the cutter in a straight line, with a cutting mat underneath to protect the mount cutter, or other surface. At this stage, don't trim the strips to the exact size of the mount, as all trimming is done at the end. The blade in the cutter can be adjusted to cut to the depth of 5mm (¼ inch). The foam core is applied to the back of the mount window in a circular fashion with a bevelled end resting against a bevelled side. In the photograph, the red cutter works anti-clockwise and the blue cutter works clockwise. For the anti-clockwise direction, the decorative tape is bound around the edge of the bevel on the left side with the bevel facing away from you, 4cm (1½ inches) in from the end. For the clockwise direction, it must be on the right, 4cm (1½ inches) in from the end. The decorative tape is very sticky, so a pencil line running 5mm (¼ inch) in from the edge of the foam core bevel will help to place it correctly first time. The first bevel strip is placed behind one side of the window to make a smooth slope inwards using masking tape rolled into a loop. The next strip is turned so that the bevel is facing towards you and placing the cutter flat on top, with a piece of mount board underneath, cut the end off, to make a bevel sloping inwards. This bevelled end will then rest against the first bevel strip to create a

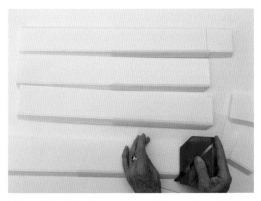

The ends of the foam core strips are bevelled using the foam core cutter.

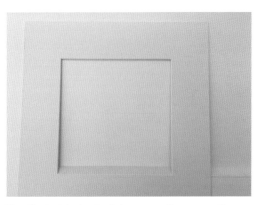

The first strip is stuck temporarily across the back of the window mount with double-sided rolls made from masking tape.

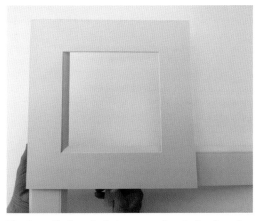

The bevelled end of the second strip is placed against the straight side of the first strip.

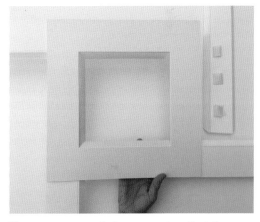

The temporary strip is removed so that the bevelled end of the third strip can be fitted.

Once the fourth strip is replaced, the excess foam core is trimmed off.

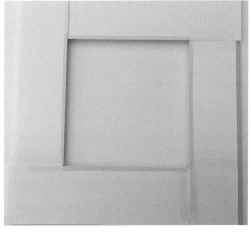

How the back of the mount should look.

Gannets trapunto embroidery designed and stitched by Lesley Hammond.

Spraying high-tack spray glue on to the mount board to attach the fabric.

corner. Fix in place with permanent double-sided tape and repeat the process with the next bevel strip, leaving the excess foam core intact. After the third strip has been cut, the first, temporary strip is taken out for the third strip to be attached. Bevel the end of the temporary strip in the same way and slot into the remaining space. Carefully trim off the excess foam core using a craft knife and ruler.

Binding the fabric around the mount board.

Fabric-covered mount

A plush effect can be achieved by adding a fabric-covered mount. Either use a mount board which has a manufactured velvet or hessian top face, usually available in a small range of colours, or a piece of fabric related to the fabric art being framed can be attached to a window mount cut with a reverse bevel. The fabric-covered mount can then be finished inside the window using a decorative slip, which will create space between the fabric art and the glass. Place a window of barrier board between the mount and the fabric art to protect the fabric art.

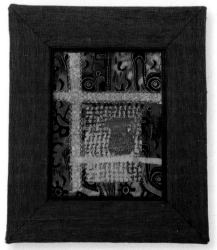

Fabric strips have been glued to an under mount and a decorative black slip added to the inside edge. Still Life designed and hand-stitched by Janet Edmonds.

Right: Frame with mount board faced-fillet to give separation from the glass.

Shadow mount and fillet spacer

The spacer can be made with a wooden fillet faced with strips of mount board, the same as used behind the fabric art, to give a complete lining to the inside of the frame. Alternatively, a thin window mount behind the glass with a strip of foam core spacer attached to the back, known as a shadow mount, can be used, which will hide the inside edges of the frame. The core of the shadow mount can be painted to accentuate a colour in the fabric. This method is described in Chapter 9.

CHOOSING THE MOULDING AND MAKING THE FRAME

The need for a large rebate depth will limit the choice of ready-finished moulding. To create extra choice, many bare wood mouldings have reasonably deep rebates and can be given a simple paint finish, or more complex as explained in Chapter 10. If a foot-operated underpinner is being used, it may be worth double banking one V nail on top of another to create a stronger join. It will be more difficult to do in hard wood, and when using a hand-operated joiner. The rebate needs to be sealed with a barrier tape to prevent sap from leaching into any fabric that comes into contact with it.

Shadow mount and complementary coloured bevel. Silk fabric art by Coral Slade.

ASSEMBLY

Assemble as outlined in Chapter 5.

Sealing the rebate with barrier tape.

HOW TO FRAME A THREE-DIMENSIONAL ITEM

ALMOST ANYTHING CAN BE FRAMED

Careful planning is needed to ensure the rebate depth of the moulding is deep enough so that the object doesn't touch the glass, and that it is strong enough to support its weight.

Deep moulding, extensions and tray frames for unglazed 3D or deep canvases.

Mounted shoes with title plaque, ready for framing.

TITLE PLAQUES

A plaque with a title or date can be placed inside with the item being framed, either in the window mount, or on the outside of the frame. If the plaque is to be placed inside, the words and letters can be scripted using a computer font, or by hand. For the outside of the frame, an engraved brass plaque is recommended.

MEASURING, CUTTING AND JOINING THE FRAME

Take measurements that allow for the width of a window mount on both sides of the viewable space with the item arranged inside, in other words viewable space and twice the width of the window mount border. Add 4mm to these measurements to allow space for a mount board lining on the depth rebate of the moulding and saw or chop the moulding, taking extra care with the rebate lip. If the rebate posts on a guillotine won't go high enough to support the rebate, place some wooden fillet inside to fill the space. Extensions can be cut separately and joined separately, then slotted together. To join the frame, glue and pin with 15mm V nails, double banking one on top of another. Place the V nails no further than 10mm from the outside edge of the frame as they can have the tendency to veer outwards as they move down into the

Measuring viewable space plus window width.

The deep moulding and extension are cut separately, and then joined together.

frame. If a hand-operated joiner is being used, two strap clamps will hold the frame together more effectively than a single clamp on two corners. If the frame is too deep to be pinned using an underpinner, then V nails can be gently tapped in using a hammer while the frame is clamped together. To secure the front of the frame beyond the reach of V nails, place some bendable metal plates inside the rebate depth and fix with counter-sunk screws.

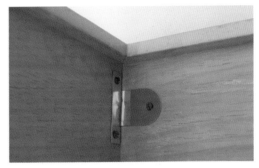

A bendable metal plate secures the top part of the moulding where the V nails cannot reach.

MULTIPLE ARRANGEMENTS

Arranging and attaching items of different thickness

The item that needs the most depth will determine the depth of rebate needed. The deep items will need a separate box within the frame, although the window mount will unite all the items in the same way as a multiple window mount. There will be unsupported cavities behind the thin items that will need bracing with foam core.

The foam core fills the space behind the window mount when framing items of different thickness.

A frame for a book with hinges, door fastening and a raised wooden plinth for the book to rest on.

ACCESSIBLE FRAMES

Some items may need to be taken out of the frame for use, and replaced afterwards. To create access, use the deep moulding upside down, with the rebate lip at the back and cut a frame to make a door which can be hinged on the front, either on the left side or the top. Backing board is placed inside first, then the mount board back and sides. The rebate depth of the door frame will need to be deep enough to accept glass and a thin fillet of wood to secure the glass inside. For this type of box a window mount is not needed.

backing board. A plinth or shelf is fixed to the bottom of the box so that the book can be raised within the frame. An upturned length of moulding cut at 45 degrees on each end serves well and will stop the book from slipping forward at the bottom. For valuable books, use conservation- or museum-grade mount board to line the box and plinth, and UV protective glass. Some books may be too fragile for upright display and are best displayed in a flat cabinet. For less valuable items, the inside could be painted with quality paint as described in Chapter 10.

Frame for a large picture book, wedding album, or antique book

If a book is simply just too big to go on a bookshelf, framing it in its own box might be the answer. Choose a moulding with sufficient depth rebate to allow the book to lean, supported against the

Frame for a collection of thimbles

Decorative thimbles can be arranged on shelving glued or screwed to a sturdy backing board, either in rows, or separately with small posts of doweling fixed into the top by drilling a hole and gluing. Choose a moulding with a suitable

An accessible frame created for a collection of thimbles by the author.

From the left: Deep moulding joined back to front; backing board; plywood with doweling rods fixed into shelving and a door frame for a collection of thimbles.

Using a wide moulding upturned to make a deep box frame.

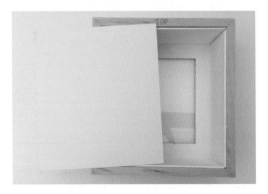

Lining a box with mount board, sides and back and with a window mount.

depth rebate and another for a door frame, assembling in the same way as the accessible frame described above.

FINISHING A BARE WOOD MOULDING

For many projects it will be necessary to create a painted or gilt effect on a bare wood moulding. Refer to Chapter 10 for ideas and methods.

USING TWO OR MORE MOULDINGS TOGETHER

Sometimes two or more mouldings can be joined one on top of another, or turned on the side, to create the extra depth and strength needed. Each frame can be cut and joined separately, then slotted together to form the complete box frame.

THE SHADOW BOX

Five piece box

Measure and cut a window mount as described in Chapters 2 and 3 . Cut a piece of mount board to line the inside of the top of the box first, allowing space for the thickness of glass, the window mount, the back mount, backing board and enough room to fix at the back with tabs. Next, measure and cut mount board to line the sides, with the top mount board in place; the sides will overlap the top board and keep it in place. Finally, cut the bottom liner which will overlap the sides, holding them in place. Mark top, ready for assembly later.

Multiple colour box

Variations for the shadow box can be made by making the window mount, side liners and back in a mixture of mount board colours and painting the bevel of the window mount, as described in Chapter 9.

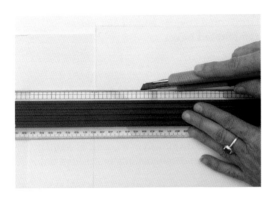

Marking and scoring the mount board.

All-in-one scored box

A window mount is cut as before. Instead of cutting the sides and back separately, a single piece of mount board is measured and cut to include the sides and back. Mark the score lines on the back and cut out the waste mount board in each corner. Score lightly along the pencil marks and fold the mount board to form a box. Tape the corners together using white self-adhesive pH-neutral tape on the back.

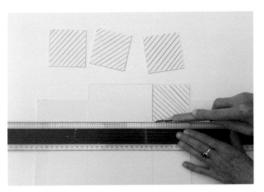

Cutting the waste mount board (slashed) out of the corners.

Taping the corners together to make the box.

A shadow mount with painted bevel to match fabric trim (see Chapter 9) completes the scored box. Marla, handmade ceramic doll circa 1991 by June Mary Bell.

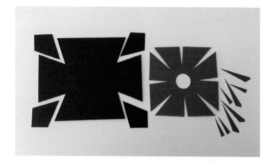

Lᴇꜰᴛ: **Scored cove or angled and more complicated boxes.**

Below: **Shell displayed in a coved or angled box. Golf ball displayed in a multisided box.**

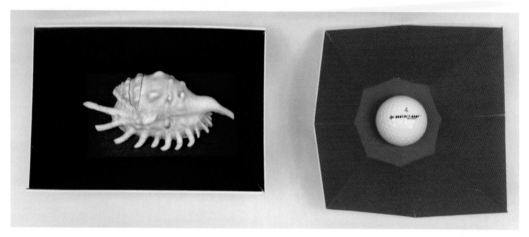

Cove or angled sides and other variations for a box

By changing the angle at which the corners are measured and cut, slanted or coved sides can be made. Measuring and scoring in this way, you can make a variety of shaped linings.

Decorative effects for a shadow box

Fabric background or fabric-faced mount board

A plush effect can be achieved by using a velvet fabric, which can be fixed to adhesive-faced foam core, or a fabric-faced mount board that is available in velvet or linen effect.

Paint effects for background, sides and window mount

Chapter 9 describes various paint effects, which may help to modify the solid, uniform look of mount board for some projects. The decoration should subtly enhance rather than distract attention from the item.

Padded fabric

A thin layer of polyester felt or wadding from a haberdashery shop is fixed to self-adhesive foam core with a fabric sewn on top like a quilt, or pinned. The padding may create a soft nest for an item that needs to lean back, such as a book, or it may be a pin board for the back of a keepsake box.

Cork

For a cabinet-style notice board, use cork with a minimum thickness of 10mm glued flat onto backing board. Depending on the size of the notice board, strips of wood will be needed to brace the back, so that when notices are pinned on, the board remains flat.

ATTACHING THE ITEM TO BE FRAMED

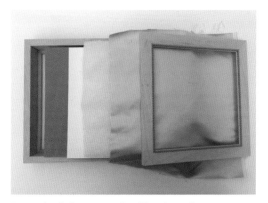

From the left: Frame, backing board, mount board, wadding, fabric and lid for a keepsake box.

Methods for fixing items need to be reversible and never cause damage to the item, therefore the use of adhesive tapes and glues in direct contact with the item is not recommended. In particular silicone adhesive will corrode metal, and other items in the frame will be affected as the adhesive continues to give off gas. Many items can be sewn to the back mount board using single stitches of a thread of appropriate weight. These are made by threading through from the back of the mount board, and through a part of the item to be framed and then back through the mount board. The threads are tied off and a piece of white self-adhesive pH-neutral tape is placed over the knot for extra security. Continue placing more single stitches as needed, taking care that they cannot be seen from the front. If the item is heavy, 10mm (½ inch) foam core faced with mount board or fabric will give extra strength. Use a combination with hefty thread, ribbon and leather straps that can be made to look decorative. Mighty Mounts are special holders available in variety of sizes and shapes to hold items and hold against the backing board by fixing securely behind.

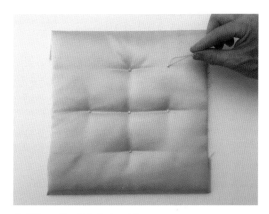

Quilting the fabric backing.

Finished keepsake box. The lid stays on with magnets.

Sewing a soft toy onto the backing.

Using a mini tag to fix doll stand to mount board.

Stuffed toys and dolls

Stuffed fabric items can be stitched onto the mount board as described above. It is best to attach items made of ceramic, plastic or wood using brackets or holders made to hold the item and fix through the mount. They can be hand-made using plastic coated wire or purchased from a supplier. A heavy item can stand on the bottom of the frame, as well as being fixed to the back. A plinth can be used to lift the item up to be seen in full view inside the shadow mount.

Medals

Medals usually have either a pin attachment or a ribbon. For a pin attachment position on the mount back, make a couple of holes with a bradawl to feed the pin into and close at the back of the mount board. It will be necessary to carve away and neaten the excess mount board around the pin attachment on each side for it to lie flat and close.

Two methods for mounting a medal attached to a ribbon are as follows.

Medals pinned through mount board. Finished with a tape-wrapped foam core bevel. For method of making the deep bevel, see Chapter 7.

Threading the ribbon through mount board.

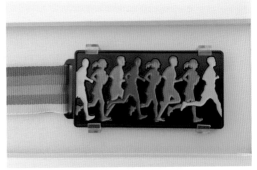

Attaching with Mighty Mounts. Medal loaned by Linda Dowell.

Mighty Mounts: Cut a small slit in the mount board the width of the ribbon and feed the end through to hold the ribbon in place. Small plastic holders called Mighty Mounts are placed around the medal, which pierce through the mount board and are fastened at the back with a small washer. They support the weight of the mount and take the strain off the ribbon.

Encapsulation using clear conservation-quality polyester film: Mark out a circle the size of the medal with radial lengths for fastening. A sharp craft knife or scalpel can be used to cut the shape out. The film can also be used to cover the ribbon with lengths of film along the sides and top for fastening. Position the medal on the front side of the mount board and mark lightly with pencil against the edge of medal, the positions where small slits will be made to feed the radial strips through. Remove the medal and cut small slits with a sharp craft knife or scalpel 5mm (¼ inch) inside the pencil mark. Make the slits from the front through to the back and trim off lumpy bits of mount board that form on the back. Feed the fastening lengths of film through the slits and place the medal underneath. When all the fastening strips have been threaded through the mount board, check that medal and ribbon are positioned correctly and pull the strips tight at the back. Lay the strips flat against the back of the mount board and tape in place using white self-adhesive pH-neutral tape.

Making a clear archival polyester cover with radial arms to hold a medal.

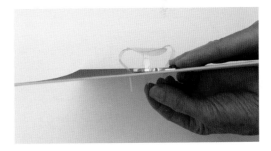

Threading the radial arms through slits in the mount board to be held in place on the back with white archival self-adhesive pH-neutral tape.

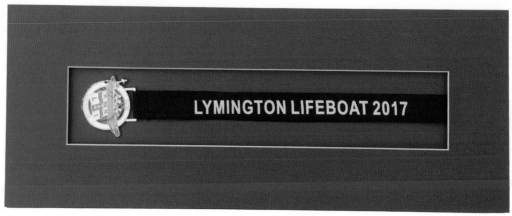

Finished medal ready for framing. Medal loaned by Linda Dowell.

Coins

Coins can be mounted in the same way as medals, either use small Mighty Mounts or encapsulate with clear conservation-quality polyester film using the same method as given for medals. Alternatively, to display both sides of the coin, it can be placed in a clear plastic coin case sandwiched between two circular window mounts cut to cover the edge of the coin case. Cut a window inside a piece of foam core for holding the coin case in place. Two frames cut the same size and glazed are then glued together back-to-back with wood glue. The thickness of the two frames combined may allow the frame to stand.

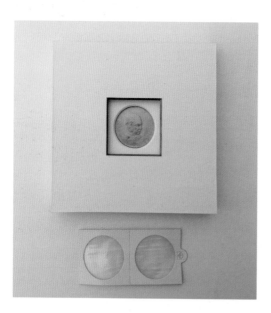

Coin held in a cardboard holder inside a foam core window sandwiched between circular and square mounts and example of a cardboard coin holder below.

Both sides of the coin can be seen in this double-sided frame held together with magnets in a stand made from the same moulding. Aluminium gilt silver finish is explained in Chapter 10.

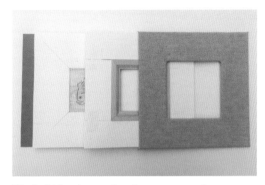

Tile held in place using foam core and a wooden slip with hemp canvas-covered reverse bevel mount.

Dance shoes fixed with top facing and side facing by threading long laces through slits in the mount board and back to the front to tie in ribbons.

Shoes

Shoes may be associated with a sport, dancing, fashion or they could be babies' or children's first shoes. They can be arranged side-on, or with the tops in full view. Wooden blocks or shelves can be attached to the back and bottom board for the shoes to rest on. Ribbons and laces may be threaded through the mount board and tied in a bow at the back.

Using Mighty Mounts to fix a plate to a mount board.

Ceramic plates and tiles

A plate can be held in place against the back board using three Mighty Mounts clips designed for plates. Plates made for display often have holes at the back for hanging, which can be used for fixing. Tiles can be secured in a tight-fit or sink mount in foam core. An additional decorative wooden slip can also be used to keep tiles from falling forwards, or they can be held with Mighty Mount clips or sometimes they may already have their own hooks. Ceramic items may be left unglazed if preferred, using a fabric-covered mount or foam board as described in Chapter 7.

Carter Tiles' Fish series by Arthur Nickols. A mount board covered with hemp canvas can be framed without glass.

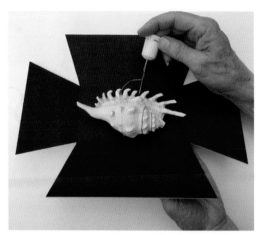

Sewing a shell onto the back board.

Shells and stones

For some shells, sewing on to the back board may be sufficient. Heavy items with no holes to pass a needle through may be rested on the bottom of a shadow box, wedged or nested in crumpled paper, or held using a Mighty Mount.

Shell/stone held in crumpled paper, or held in using small window cuts on all sides.

Vinyl record or compact disc and cover

Long-play vinyl records can be attached to the back mount board using upholstery tacks, brass paper fasteners or binder screws. Short play vinyl records will need flat-hole converter discs, which snap into the centre to make the hole the same size as that in a long-play vinyl record. Compact discs can be attached using an all-purpose holder made by Mighty Mount, or the back of a compact disc case attached to the mount backing board.

Record covers can be attached using L-shaped corner holders made from clear conservation-quality polyester film taped onto the backing board. A sink mount as described in Chapter 2 would display and keep a plastic compact disc case in place. A vinyl record and case, or a com-

Attaching a single vinyl record and using L-shaped corners to attach the cover.

pact disc and case can be framed with or without a window mount. A window mount can also echo the shape of the case and disc by using an arch.

Sports paraphernalia

Boxing glove

A boxing glove can be attached to the back mount board by making two holes large enough to thread the laces and tying in a bow at the back. Another fixing point can be made by making two more holes in the back mount board further down and threading wire or heavy thread through the laces. Tie off the thread and tape down with white pH-neutral self adhesive tape or wind the wires around each other. Laces can be tied in a bow. A foam core layer placed behind the back mount board will give extra strength as needed.

Ball

Cut a circle to the diameter of the ball and make a supporting box at the back out of 10mm (½ inch) foam core to hold the ball in place. If the ball is stitched together, thread can be looped through stitches, passed through the mount board back, tied off and taped as described above.

Cricket bat or golf iron

Sew with single stitches of thread around the handle through the mount backing board and foam for added strength, tie off and tape over the thread with white pH-neutral self-adhesive tape. The bottom can be sunk into the bottom of the box slightly by cutting a small window of mount board and making a small supporting box at the back out of 10mm foam core. The handle can then be secured discreetly with loops of thread or wire, or mini cable ties secured through the backing mount board.

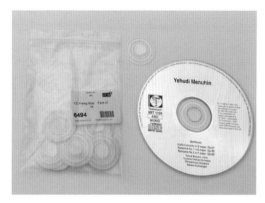

Attaching a compact disc with a compact disc holder.

Threading laces through the mount board and fastening with a bow.

Boxing glove. The glove is lifted forward by the POW symbol, which is supported on 10mm thick foam core.

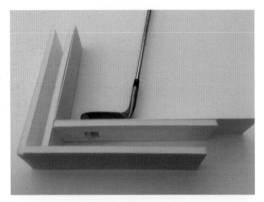

Foam core support for the bottom of a golf club.

As it will appear in a window mount.

Mighty Mounts are also available for cricket bats and golf irons.

Sports cap

To keep the shape of the cap, stuff with pH-neutral tissue paper and sew on as described above.

Sports T-shirt

Sports shirts are often made of nylon aertex; the mount board shaper needs to be the same colour as the T-shirt so it won't show through. The shirt is attached to the backing mount board at the neck, outer shoulder, armpits and bottom with loops of thread, tied off at the back and finished with white pH-neutral tape.

Red mount board shaper to go inside the T-shirt.

Attaching at the neck.

Attaching at the shoulder.

Attaching at the armpits.

Dried flowers stuck into dry flower Oasis.

Dried wedding bouquet in a box frame.

Dried flowers

Flowers may be saved from a memorable occasion such as a wedding bouquet or hair decoration. They need to be thoroughly dried and a desiccant silica gel sachet concealed inside the box frame to help protect the flowers from condensation. Flower stems can be inserted into dry flower Oasis, which is a pale beige colour. Any flowers that are falling apart may be wired or pinned and rotten stalks can be replaced with stainless steel pins.

ASSEMBLY AND DISPLAY

Follow the procedures for assembly and display methods as explained in Chapter 5.

In addition some fixings behind the mount board may need extra space. Cut a thick sheet of foam core with windows cut out to house the fixings and prevent them from getting crushed when the final backing board is placed. If the backing board is removed in the future it will be easy to see the fixing method, should anyone wish to remove the objects from the box.

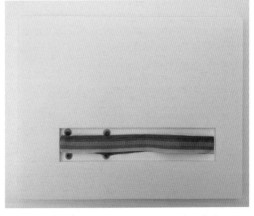

Allowing three-dimensional space for fixings at the back of the frame.

HOW TO CREATE DECORATIVE EFFECTS ON MOUNTS USING PAINT AND METAL LEAF

PAINT, INK, PASTEL AND METAL LEAF COLOURS

Acrylic paint

Ordinary artists'- or student-quality acrylic paint is available in a wide range of colours, including silver, gold and bronze. It will dry quickly allowing another layer to be added without disturbing the layer underneath.

Watercolour paint

Use an artists'-quality watercolour that will be more resistant to fading, available in tubes or tablets. Only small amounts of paint are needed for subtle translucent paint effects.

Applying soft pastel with a sponge brush.

Designers' gouache paint

Gouache paint is similar to watercolour but much heavier and opaque in consistency. It is best used in a single layer for achieving hard-edged, solid areas of colour.

Pastel or powdered pigments

Use artists'-quality soft pastels that are powdery to the touch and easy to grate. A box of pastels allows easy selection from a range of colours, or use the original pigments in powdered form (the raw pigments used for making all paint colours).

Soft pastel border on a watercolour painting by the author.

The pigment is rubbed onto the surface using a dry sponge brush or rag and the excess powder is removed by lifting with a clean dry sponge to avoid it becoming airborne. Pastel can be fixed with a light spray of pastel fixative. Cover the outside area of the mount with a strip of mount board while spraying.

Applying gold metal leaf to letters painted with acrylic size.

Metallic ink

Metallic inks can be acrylic based, water soluble, or spirit based in a range of colours such as silver, copper, bronze and gold. They are used in a lining pen to make decorative lines around the window mount for traditional line and watercolour wash.

Gold, silver and metal leaf flakes

Spray, print or paint a design in glue size and apply the gold or metal leaf, patting down and sweeping the excess off with a stiff round brush. Double-sided tape can be used to create clean, straight lines. After positioning the tape, lift off the backing

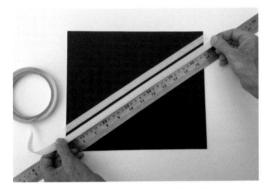

Applying a diagonal line of double-sided tape onto black mount board.

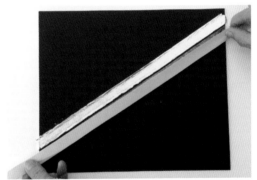

Applying a diagonal line of metal leaf onto black mount board.

Brushing the excess metal leaf away.

Classic sports car.

Applying metal leaf flakes onto a border of double-sided tape.

Brushing the excess gold flakes away.

and apply the gold either in large or small leaf. Brush in and remove the excess as before.

SAFETY AND PERMANENCE

Colour pigments behave differently, the effect will be more noticeable in watercolour paint and some are more prone to fading. Many pigments are toxic, so they will need to be handled with care in the powder form. Wash hands after use and don't allow them to become airborne.

MOUNT COLOUR AND SURFACE TEXTURE

Acrylic paint used at tube consistency is opaque enough to cover any type of mount colour and surface. Metal leaf gilding can look very effective on dark colours as well as the paler mount colours, though smooth mount board might be a better choice, as textured will be exaggerated by the metal. Watercolour paint looks best and at its brightest when used on white- or cream-coloured mount board. Use conservation- or museum-quality mount board so that the bevel on the window does not go brown with age.

For some effects such as line and wash, stencilling and masking, smooth mount board will be easier to use.

TECHNIQUES FOR APPLYING PAINT, INK, METAL LEAF AND PASTEL

Masking and stencilling

Masking
Areas of the window mount can be masked off with removable Sellotape. Paint can be applied using some of the following techniques or apply artists' soft pastel grated finely, or powdered pigments rubbed on with a rag or sponge brush.

Art masking gum
Free-form patterns can be drawn onto the window mount using liquid masking fluid applied using a thin stick, the end of a brush, or a brush kept for the purpose. Allow the gum to dry completely before applying either acrylic or gouache paint in a thin wash all over, or watercolour paint. Wait until the paint is fully dry, then peel away the gum by rubbing with the ball of your thumb to reveal crisp lines of unpainted mount board.

Applying paint to a masked border.

Removing the Scotch 811 removable tape.

Applying art masking gum in a random pattern on a masked border.

Stencilling

Ready-made stencils can be used to make random patterns or borders. Self-adhesive reusable glass stencils stick to the mount board and a perfect stencil can be made using undiluted gouache or acrylic paint applied with a small, flat nylon brush. To make unique patterns, use a fine blade or scalpel to cut patterns in polyester Mylar stencil film or take your designs to a commercial stencil cutter.

Applying paint over the dried gum.

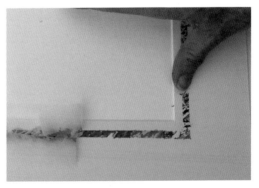

Rubbing the art masking gum away after the paint has dried.

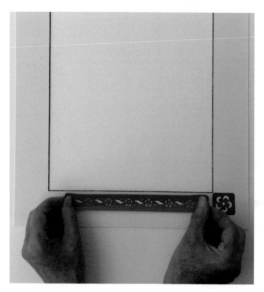

Applying a reusable sticky stencil to the mount border.

Applying acrylic paint through the stencil with a brush.

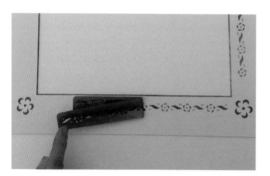

Peeling the stencil away, once the paint has dried.

Stencilled mount border.

Sponging, ragging and stippling

Sponging

A textured effect can be created with sponge, ranging from fine to broad using plastic and natural sponges. A dry sponge will give a more defined pattern. Squeeze out excess water, dip in paint and apply in bouncing movements to the surface of the mount board. As the first colour dries, further colours can be added.

Ragging

Soft cotton rag can used in a similar way to sponge and for a smoother effect, press and rub the paint onto and away from the board.

Removing the tape.

Stippling paint onto a masked border.

Applying watercolour with a sponge.

Finished decorative mount. Artwork *Princess Party* by Barbara McCardle.

Stippling

Stippling is done with a stiff brush, either a stippling brush or an artists' hog hair brush. Pick paint up on the tip of the brush and apply in bouncing movements, adding more colour layers as they dry.

Printing

Printed patterns can be made by laying undiluted acrylic, gouache paint or ink onto a design block using a flat nylon brush and printing randomly, or within masked areas. Anything with a raised surface can be used to hold the paint or ink, even the veins in the back of a leaf will give an interesting pattern.

Printing with a small stamp in designers' gouache paint.

Marking the positions using a pencil and corner-marking gauge.

Loading the lining pen with watercolour paint.

Traditional watercolour, gouache, gold ink ruling and watercolour wash

Line and watercolour wash are the perfect presentation for watercolour paintings, but they can also look good around some photographs such as old sepia or black and white prints. Mark light pencil points on each corner of the window mount using a corner gauge. Traditionally the lines are marked from the top edge of the window bevel at 5 or 8mm (¼ or ⅜ of an inch), with a band of colour measuring 12 or 18mm (½ or ¾ inches) wide. No more than half the mount is decorated. Mix watercolour or gouache into a liquid consistency and place a small amount inside the tip of a lining pen opened to the required line width, using a brush. Use a ruler that is slightly raised to prevent the liquid from seeping underneath and draw lines from mark to mark, tilting the pen slightly in the direction the pen is moving. Reload the pen each time using small amounts of paint or ink to avoid the liquid leaking as it is used. A variety of lines can be arranged in colours that relate to the artwork and a broad area of watercolour wash can be applied between two lines. Apply with a watercolour brush onto the previously dampened board to allow the paint to spread evenly.

Making a watercolour line.

Applying a watercolour wash between the lines.

Making a gold line.

Traditional line and wash mount for a watercolour. Artwork by the author.

PAINTED WINDOW MOUNT

Continuation of the artwork onto the mount

An unusual and unique effect can be achieved by extending the artwork style, subject or even the same media onto the window mount. A watercolour artist may extend the outside edges of their painting to give the effect of continuation. Themed decorative details could be used for photographs. Create a window mount slip as described in variations for a double mount in Chapter 6. This thin slip of mount on the outside of the window mount will keep the artwork on the mount away from the glass.

Printed leaves extend over the mount border with thin mount board slip on the outside edge. Artwork by the author.

PAINTED BEVELS

Draw the cutting lines for a window mount, and mark their positions on the edge of the front of the mount board. Scotch 811 removable tape is then placed on the front of the mount board on the line where the window will be cut. Press down firmly and cut the window out. The bevel can then be painted easily without paint going on the front face of the mount board. Use acrylic, gouache, gold ink or metallic framer filler, which can be buffed on with a rag. It works best on smooth mount board because the tape doesn't adhere well to textured mount board and allows the paint to leach underneath. Allow the paint to dry and then peel away the tape to reveal a perfect painted bevel.

Applying Scotch 811 removable tape to the front of the mount board in line with the pencil borders before cutting the window.

Applying paint with a sponge to the bevel edge.

Or stippling paint with a brush to the bevel edge.

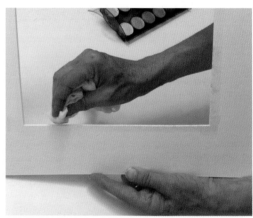

Or applying paint with a rag to the bevel edge.

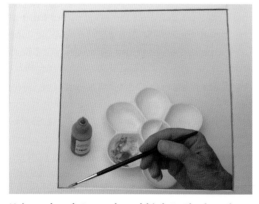

Using a brush to apply gold ink to the bevel edge.

Removing the Scotch 811 tape to reveal the painted bevel.

DECORATION ON OTHER MOUNT STYLES

Double mount with paint effect

Select two mount board colours, bearing in mind that the bottom mount will have a paint effect. Acrylic, watercolour or gouache paint can then be applied to the bottom mount using the application techniques described above. Once the paint is dry, follow the procedure given in Chapter 6 for creating a double mount. After the mount is cut the bevel can also be painted, or left white.

Applying a paint effect onto the bottom mount.

Painted faux double or inlay mount

Plan a single window mount allowing for extra width around for the inlay and the window. Keeping the fallout in place, draw some pencil registration marks across the cuts for realigning later. Separate the fallout and apply a paint effect as described above on the outside edges to cover the planned width of the inlay. Allow the paint to dry and then replace back into the window, realigning the registration marks. Tape together on the back of the board using white pH-neutral self-adhesive tape and then draw and cut the final window size. After removing the second fallout, the bevel edge can be painted or left white.

Applying paint to the bevelled edge.

Painted V groove

Follow the procedure for making a V groove in Chapter 6 and before cutting each side of the V groove, place Scotch 811 removable tape on the front side of the mount board over the line of the cut. Cut both sides of the V groove and apply a paint effect. Allow the paint to dry before removing the tape and assembling.

Double mount with painted bottom mount. Artwork by the author.

Applying a paint effect to the edge of the fallout.

Faux double mount with painted inside border. Artwork by the author.

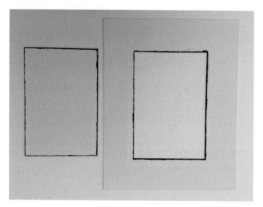

The V groove border is masked with Scotch 811 removable tape and cut out. The edges are painted after the fallout has been trimmed.

Painted V groove border. Artwork by the author.

HOW TO REPAIR MINOR DAMAGE TO MOUNTS

Paint drips

Drips made when using watercolour can be removed by wetting a brush in deionized water, squeezing it out and gently lifting the paint off the surface. Pat the surface dry with a clean, absorbent rag.

Allow acrylic paint drips to dry thoroughly then gently scrape them away using a scalpel or new sharp blade and clean eraser. A magnifying glass is helpful for seeing exactly where to scrape.

Marks

Pencil marks can be removed with a putty rubber. Sometimes marks can appear to be embedded in the surface of the mount board. Using the tip of a scalpel, or the corner of a new mount-cutting blade, gently loosen and then lift out with putty rubber.

HOW TO CREATE DECORATIVE EFFECTS ON FRAMES USING PAINT, DYE, WAX AND METAL LEAF

CHOOSING A MOULDING

Profile

Ridged moulding can be used to separate colours, patterns and gilded areas. Gullies can collect paint, dye or wax to intensify their effect. Plain flat, scoop, cassetta and reverse bevel mouldings are suitable for overall continuous gilding, patterns or paint effects.

Wood

Obeche, with its fine grain and smooth surface, is a good choice for applying many of the following paint and gilding effects described here. It is available in a wide range of profiles. Oak, ash, pine and beech generally only need a minimal treatment of wax to enhance the natural beauty of their grain.

QUICK AND SIMPLE DECORATIVE EFFECTS

These quick and simple effects can be applied to the moulding before or after being joined. An advantage gained in applying the effects after joining is that a perfect seamless join can be made by filling any gaps with wood filler and careful sanding with fine sand paper before applying paint, dye and wax.

Examples of ridged moulding.

MAKING AND USING WOOD FILLER

Squeeze out a little wood glue and mix some sawdust to make a stiff paste. Apply the wood filler to gaps using a strip of mount board and scrape off any excess from the surface of the frame. Let the filler dry and clean any remaining filler from the surface of the frame using fine grade sandpaper.

Applying wood filler made with glue and sawdust mixed to a stiff dough.

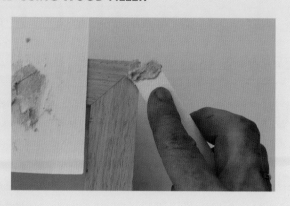

Brushing with a wire brush to 'open' the grain for accepting liming wax.

Lime wax

Lime wax is made from lime, wax and a solvent and is translucent, so when choosing the moulding avoid dark marks or knots, as they will be accentuated rather than covered. Open the grain of the wood with a wire brush, using gentle sweeps along the frame to include the sight edge, top and side of the moulding. Apply the lime wax with a soft cloth, rubbing thoroughly into the grain and buff the surface. It will dry in about twenty minutes depending on how thickly it is applied.

SAFETY ADVICE

Use lime wax, spirit dyes and varnish in a well-ventilated space and wear latex gloves, especially if skin is sensitive. These products cannot easily be washed off hands or clothing.

Applying liming wax.

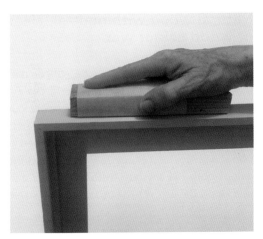

Sanding the frame with fine sand paper.

Applying an undercoat of paint.

Sanding the frame between coats of paint.

Applying smooth coats of acrylic paint.

Paint or dye

Paint

For a uniform painted frame, use a quick-drying water-based undercoat, then smooth, even layers of a good quality interior water-based paint. Allow to dry between each layer and sand with fine sand paper to remove brush marks.

Dye

Use either water- or spirit-based dye depending on the type of wood. Generally, hard woods need spirit dye as it is more easily absorbed into the wood. A wax or varnish is applied on top once it is dry, to seal the surface.

Finished frame. *Fibre Paste Flowers*, acrylic painting by Elaine Scott.

Applying a water-based wood dye.

Lime wax over paint or dye

Give the frame a light sanding, paint with acrylic paint or wood dye first and let it dry thoroughly before rubbing lime wax over the top. Rub back the lime wax to a thin surface coat to reveal the coloured layer underneath.

Applying liming wax on top of acrylic paint.

Natural wood with neutral, clear or wood colour wax

Many bare wood mouldings can be left their natural colour or given a slight translucent change in colour using oak, walnut or mahogany colour waxes to enhance natural variations such as knots and ring lines. The wood will naturally darken in colour with age and exposure to light. Sand the wood lightly, fill any gaps with wood filler and then apply the wax with a rag, buffing to a shine.

Applying a clear wax to an ash frame.

Dye with gilt cream highlights

Dye the made-up frame or moulding using a water-based or spirit dye allowing it to dry thoroughly, then apply gilt cream on raised edges of the moulding or lightly buff into the grain of the wood using a rag. A little clear wax will help the gilt cream to spread evenly.

Applying gilt cream to the raised decoration on top of a dyed frame.

MORE COMPLEX DECORATIVE EFFECTS

Preparing a wood surface

Lightly sand the surface of the wood to smooth, taking care not to over-sand a decorative profile. If the frame is made before applying the finish, it will allow the opportunity to sand or fill any gaps in the corners of the frame. If the frame is to be gilded with metal or gold leaf, a coat of rabbit-skin size is then applied to allow subsequent layers of gesso to adhere. The rabbit-skin glue creates a flexible layer that can expand and contract with the wood. If a paint effect is going to be applied it may only be necessary to apply a primer paint or acrylic size to seal the wood, and resin sealer if wood resin is likely to leach through the paint layers.

Applying rabbit-skin glue size.

> **USING BLOCKS TO RAISE THE FRAME**
>
> Before applying glue size, gesso and paint, place the frame or moulding on narrow wood blocks to raise it above the work surface to prevent size, gesso or paint from gluing the frame to the work surface and allowing smooth run-off on the edges.

Rabbit-skin glue

Preparing the glue

Soak grains of rabbit-skin glue at a rate of 45gm (1½oz) in 750ml (1¼ pints) warm water overnight and then gently warm in a double saucepan or bain-marie until it is free of lumps. Strain out any lumps if necessary. A small spoonful of chalk whiting can be dropped into the glue, allowing it to settle on the bottom before mixing. This small amount of whiting will help the following gesso layers to bond to the surface. A fresh batch of skin

glue will need to be made for each project, as the glue will lose its strength and go mouldy in a few days.

Applying the glue

Using a sash brush or artists' hog brush, apply the glue in long, even sweeps on the sight edge, top and side of the moulding and work it into any crevices. The glue layer needs at least twenty-four hours to fully dry and soak into the wood before applying gesso and if another coat is needed, allow another twenty-four hours. Working in a warm room will assist the drying process. Finally sand off any rough areas before applying gesso.

Gesso layers

Preparing the gesso

Make warm glue size as before and drop spoonfuls of whiting at a rate of 1 part to 1 part in weight and let it sink to the bottom to remove air and lumps. The gesso should be the consistency of thin cream for crevices and fine detail and it can be made a little thicker for flat areas to reduce the number of coats needed.

Applying the gesso

Stipple the first coat of gesso onto the surface to create better adhesion, then apply thin layers using a broad brush to obtain smooth layers. Use

Applying gesso.

Applying thick gesso through a polyester stencil.

The stencil is lifted to reveal the textured gesso.

is completely dry it can be sanded smooth with fine sand paper and wiped clean with a damp cotton cloth. Any rough areas will be accentuated by metal or gold leaf. A rough texture can be created deliberately by embossing or combing the last coat of gesso or embedding textured materials onto it.

A plastic comb is dragged through thick gesso to create a textured pattern.

Pressing patterns onto thick gesso.

Embedding net curtain onto a frame with gesso.

a smaller brush for crevices and moulded detail. Allow each layer to tack dry, twenty minutes to half an hour before applying the next layer. For water gilding, about six to eight layers can be applied to create a very smooth surface, though care is needed with intricate shaped moulding so that the design is not obscured by the gesso. For a painted surface, two or three coats of gesso may be sufficient. The gesso will also need to be cleared from the corners of the sight edge where it has a tendency to build up. When the gesso

Applying thin acrylic paint into gullies to bring out texture.

Bole layers (coloured clay)

Preparing the bole

Select the bole colour according to the choice of metal leaf or gold to be applied. Red bole is generally used under real gold and is suitable for burnishing, as it is harder than the other colours. Yellow bole is used as well as red for moulded patterns, as it blends in if any areas and crevices get missed in the gilding process. Black or yellow looks attractive under silver or aluminium. The clay bole is finely grated into a powder, ground with a muller and moistened with warm rabbit-skin size at a rate of six parts of size to one part of bole so that the consistency is like milk.

Sanding gesso coat.

Applying the bole

Apply two layers of bole in smooth, even strokes, allowing it to tack dry in between coats. The bole layer can be sanded or, if using red bole, it can also be burnished to a shine using an agate stone.

Applying red clay bole.

Applying yellow clay bole.

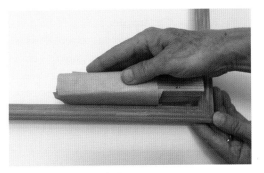

Sanding the red bole layer.

GILDING

Water gilding

A gilders' cushion and knife are often used to lay leaves of gold out and cut to size, then a gilders' tip which is a thin, wide badger brush is used to pick up the gold sheets and lay them onto the pre-wetted surface of the clay bole. The bole is wetted with gilders' size, which is made with half a teaspoon of rabbit-skin size added to half a pint (300ml) of distilled water and 2 to 3 dessert spoons of isopropyl alchohol. The size draws the gold onto the clay and needs to be used fresh. Later, the gold can be burnished to a shine using an agate stone.

Oil gilding

The smoothed surface of the frame is painted with gold size using an ox hair or sable brush. Gold size is a linseed-based size with a drying time between two and sixteen hours, depending on the warmth of the room. The longer the size takes to dry the better it can level and smooth out the brush marks, which will otherwise show through the gilding. The size will have developed the right amount of tack when it looks dull and a knuckle lightly dragged on the side of the frame will make a squeaky sound. There is a danger that impression marks can be made in the size when it is still not quite ready. Either loose leaf or transfer real gold or metal leaf can be used. Real gold or metal leaf, which has been pressed onto transfer paper, is easier for beginners to cut and apply. Loose pieces of metal leaf can be picked up on transfer paper and used to fill any areas that get missed. Gold size can be used to draw patterns onto moulding as shown in the following example.

Applying gilding size to the boled ornament. (Photo: Joseph McCarthy Fine Frames Ltd.)

Applying gold leaf with a gilders' tip (brush). (Photo: Joseph McCarthy Fine Frames Ltd.)

Burnishing the gold leaf with an agate stone. (Photo: Joseph McCarthy Fine Frames Ltd.)

Gilding with acrylic size

Acrylic size, called Wundersize, is easy to use for beginners to apply metal or real gold attached to transfer paper. A little water can be added for smooth application with a nylon brush. The size is ready in about fifteen minutes, when it looks transparent and is tacky. It will remain permanently sticky, therefore is unsuitable for burnishing real gold.

Painting a pattern onto the frame using gold size.

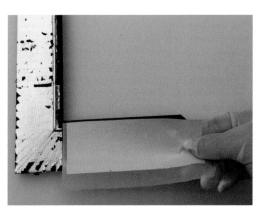

Applying metal leaf.

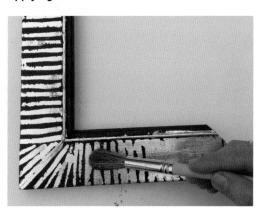

Sweeping off the loose metal.

Applying acrylic size.

Applying aluminium silver transfer leaf metal.

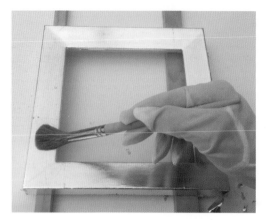

Brushing the surplus metal leaf away.

Applying acrylic size to missed areas.

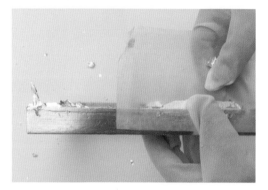

Applying metal leaf to missed areas.

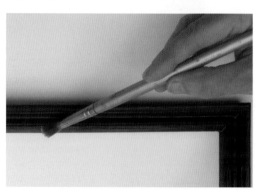

Applying acrylic size onto a painted frame.

Gilding flakes

Gilding flakes are made of imitation gold, silver or bronze. Apply a gold or acrylic size such as Wundersize and wait until it is tack dry before sprinkling the flakes on and patting them onto the size. Sweep off loose flakes with a brush and seal with a varnish or gold size.

Applying metal leaf flakes.

Applying paint and gilt varnish

Paint can be used alone on top of gesso for a smooth finish, underneath or on top of gold and metal leaf, or gilt varnish. Artists' acrylic paint is versatile, easy to use and quick to dry. It may be necessary to experiment to get the consistency right when it is mixed with water, as too much water will cause the paint to bubble and run.

Sweeping the surplus flakes away.

Finished frame with a coat of coloured varnish to match the picture.

A little colour theory

For a striking effect, use complementary opposite colours in separate paint applications, or if a colour is too strong, use a thin wash of its complementary opposite colour to neutralize it. Examples of complementary opposite pairs are red and green, blue and orange, purple and yellow, black and white. As well as bright colours around the colour circle, some earthy colours such as Burnt Sienna, Umber and Yellow Ochre can be used straight from the tube to reduce the amount of colour mixing needed. Gold, silver and bronze acrylic paint will give a shiny glow applied on top of other colours.

Masking

Allow foundation coats of paint or gesso to dry completely first. Use masking tape or removable tape to mask areas of the frame, either along the length or across the width. Press the edges of the tape firmly to prevent paint from seeping underneath. Paint can now be applied to the exposed areas using any of the following methods.

Spraying and flicking

Thin artists' acrylic paint to a consistency that will allow it to be picked up on a stiff toothbrush and make a fine spray over the surface of the frame.

Mixing complementary colours together.

Spraying thin acrylic paint with a toothbrush.

Applying acrylic paint with a sponge.

Applying paint to a masked-off area of the frame.

Applying acrylic paint with a stiff brush.

Allow the paint to dry and re-spray with another colour. Allow the paint to dry before each new coat of paint. Long splash marks can be made across the surface of the frame by flicking the paint, using a long artists' brush dipped in liquid acrylic paint.

Sponging and ragging

Natural and synthetic sponges can be dipped in tube-consistency acrylic paint, or use a brush to lay the colour over the sponge. Bounce the sponge over the surface of the frame. Rinse the paint out of the sponge thoroughly between each coat. A softer effect can be achieved when the sponge is damp. A soft cotton rag can be used in a similar way, using the rag to rub paint onto the surface and rub off for a subtle effect as used by interior decorators.

Brushing and stippling

Use soft, nylon brushes for a smooth, even paint layer with tube-consistency or slightly wetted paint. Brush effects can be obtained by using stiff brushes such as artists' hog hair. For a stippled effect dip a stiff brush or stippling brush into paint, clean some of the paint from the brush and stipple over the surface of the frame. Gilt varnish can be applied over paint layers using this method for a bright effect.

Flicked, or splashed paint patterns.

Stencilling with acrylic paint.

Leaf printing with acrylic paint.

Printing and stencilling

Anything with a raised, textured surface can be used as a printing tool. Apply tube-consistency paint across the surface of the printing tool, using a soft brush, then press onto the frame surface and lift off. Examples of raised textured surfaces are bubble wrap, a thin scrunched plastic bag, the veined backs of leaves or patterned printing blocks. Stick-on or hold-down stencils can be used to paint all sorts of designs onto a flat or cassetta frame using tube-consistency paint.

Using a printing block with acrylic paint.

Bubble wrap printing with acrylic paint.

Scrunched plastic printing with acrylic paint.

Distressing a textured frame.

Applying gilt cream over acrylic paint to 'mellow' the paint effect.

Distressing

An aged effect can be given to a gilded or painted surface by intentionally rubbing some of the surface finish away to reveal coats of bole or paint underneath. Use fine grade wire wool in gentle circular movements so that the wear effect looks even, or for a classic swept pasta-style frame, the raised design can be gently rubbed.

Varnishes and rottenstone

A final coat of varnish will seal the paint and give a gloss or matt finish. Real gold does not need sealing as it won't tarnish, although real silver and metal leaf will, so both need sealing. A little paint or pigment added to gold size can be used as a varnish, and at the same time to soften the colour of metal leaf. Rottenstone is dusted on using a stiff brush and allowed to collect in crevices for an aged effect.

Applying gold size mixed with a little oil paint to 'mellow' the brash foil colour.

MULTI-PIECE, PASTA AND HAND-MOULDED FRAMES

Multi-piece frames

Multi-piece frames can be made by adding slips to widen the frame, or create a unique frame. Cut and assemble the moulding and slip separately, then glue and pin them together. Afterwards they can be gilded and painted as one piece.

Applying rottenstone to 'mellow' the gold colour.

Pasta moulding

The raised pattern of pasta moulding is perfect for applying gilding or paint effects as the pattern is accentuated when paint gathers in the gullies of the design. Raised areas can be distressed or highlighted with gilt varnish or cream.

Applying gilt varnish on the raised pattern of a pasta moulding.

Hand-moulded frames

Known as classical swept frames. Corner patterns and patterns along the length of the frame are modelled and cast in a resin and plaster mix. They are glued onto a wooden base frame and finished with gilding and paint effects.

HOW TO REPAIR DAMAGE TO A PICTURE FRAME

Broken or cracked corners

Feed wood glue into the corners, pushing it all the way down as far as possible. Then clamp the frame using a good quality strap clamp. Place small pieces of mount board between the frame and the clamp to prevent the clamp from denting the frame on the outside corners. Leave the clamped frame aside to harden the glue. Metal L-plates can be placed on the corners at the back of the frame for extra strength.

Chipped corners

Fill with wood filler, level and smooth the surface and leave to dry. Sand smooth if necessary and apply paint to match the frame, or gilt cream in gold and silver to match gold or silver frames.

Classical hand-crafted frame. (Photo: Joseph McCarthy Fine Frames Ltd.)

Dents

If the moulding is still bare wood, a dent can be steamed out, as the wood fibres will regain their shape. If the frame has any type of finish, minor damage can be filled with wood filler and repainted, but matching colours and gilding are tricky. It may be necessary to repaint or gild the entire frame as an upcycling project.

Missing resin decoration

Make a mould from a good part of the frame and cast it with plaster coloured to match the frame. After it is dry, trim to fit and glue in place.

UPCYCLING AN OLD FRAME

Re-sizing

It is preferable to avoid cutting the frame down in size because of the risk of damaging blades on hidden nails. However if it is unavoidable, use a powerful magnet to detect any hidden metal within the frame and cut with a saw, as it is less expensive to replace than the blades in a mitre guillotine or mitre trimmer.

Preparing the surface

Sand the surface of the frame to remove varnish, flaking paint or gilding. Use wire wool to clean in crevices. Old gesso can be removed by placing damp sand on the surface overnight to soften it. Depending on how the frame was decorated, it may be necessary to clean back as far as the wood, or to a gesso or bole layer, all of which could provide an absorbent surface for a new coat of paint, gesso, or gilding as long as they are stable.

GLOSSARY

Bain-marie is a saucepan with two walls. Warm water can be poured between the walls so that the contents can be heated gently.

Bevel (biseau); angled cut sloping toward artwork on a mount.

Blue wool scale is used for measuring and calibrating the permanence of inks, dyes and colour pigments.

Bole; the coloured clay layer between the gesso and final gold or metal leaf. There are different qualities and attributes according to the colour and origin of the clay.

Burnish; to rub and smooth a surface to create a shine. An agate stone is used, particularly on real gold water-gilding.

Core; inside pulp of paper-faced mount board, which is mostly white.

Distressed; an artificially created effect of age and wear achieved by sanding or polishing with fine sand paper or a fine grade wire wool.

Dutch metal is imitation gold or silver leaf made from base metals such as copper and zinc. It is easier to handle than real gold, as it is thicker and less prone to breaking.

Fallout; the piece of mount board in the centre that is discarded when cutting a window mount.

Gesso is Italian for chalk. For building a smooth surface on a frame, the chalk, or whiting (calcium carbonate) is bound with warm rabbit-skin glue.

Gilding is the art of applying real gold or metal leaf to a prepared surface.

Glass size is the external measurement of the window mount.

Mellowing; to soften the brash effect of a newly gilded frame using various methods.

Micron is the unit used for measuring the thickness of mount board. One micron is equal to one millimetre.

Mount board (mat board); specially made pulp or cotton board for picture framing.

Moulding (molding) is shaped lengths of wood with rebates for holding the components of a picture frame.

Oil gilding; the use of an oil-based gold size to stick the gold or metal leaf.

Rebate depth (rabbit) is the inside measurement of the moulding from front to back.

Rebate lip is the small overhang on the inside edge of moulding which holds the contents of the frame in.

Rebate size is the external measurement of the window mount plus an extra 2 to 3mm to allow for expansion of the materials inside.

Rottenstone is a mineral powder generally used for cleaning, but framers use it to create an aged effect when applied to the crevices of a classical swept frame.

Reverse bevel; cut in the opposite direction to remove sight of the core.

Sight edge is the inside edge of the frame which may be decorated with gold.

Stencil is a pattern cut out of a sheet of plastic or some other material.

Warp and weft; in plain weave, weft threads are interlaced across warp threads at 90 degrees to make fabric.

Water gilding is when the gold or metal leaf is laid onto the wetted bole layer.

Whiting is finely ground chalk for making gesso.

Window mount (passe-partout); mount board frame around artwork.

Window size is the viewable image size.

LIST OF CONTRIBUTORS

Alfamacchine Italy
Alexandra Zillweger, *Ladies*, colour drawings.
Barbara McArdle, *Princess Party*, watercolour and collage.
Charnwood UK.
Elaine Barr, *Woodpecker and Robin*, cross stitching.
Elaine Scott, *Fibre Paste Flowers*, acrylic painting.
Heritage Crafts Ltd UK.
Janet Edmonds, *Still Life*, hand-stitched fabric.

June Bell, *Marla*, handmade ceramic doll.
Karen Rees in *Chasing the Ferries*, photograph by Jonathan Tribbeck.
Linda Dowell, medals and photograph by Graeme Stringer.
Logan Graphic Products, Inc. USA.
Matty Smith, *Urban Reflections*, tapestry.

FURTHER INFORMATION

COURSES

UK School of Framing at allaboutframing.com
Supply a comprehensive range of courses from the basics of framing for complete beginners through to master classes and business development training.

Fine Art Trade Guild
Training, exam qualifications and meetings around the UK, which allow the framer to keep up with the latest standards set for the picture framing industry.

BOOKS

The Library of Professional Picture Framing
Six volumes of in-depth guides on various aspects of picture framing illustrated with drawings and black and white photographs by professional American picture framer Vivian C. Kistler CPF (Certified Picture Framer) of the Professional Picture Framers Association (PPFA).

Fine Art Trade
Provide training manuals for exams, which contain up-to-date information on framing methods and best practice. www.fineart.co.uk

Practical Gilding
A good practical guide on gilding by Peter and Ann Mactaggart. Published by Mac & Me Ltd, England, 1984.

The Art of Decorative Matting
A detailed step-by-step guide on how to create traditional French line and wash decoration for window mounts by Sylvie Robin. Translated from French to English in 1997 by Josh Heuman and published by Lyons and Burford.

YOUTUBE

Gilding course by Rinaldin
Eleven videos including an introduction, demonstrating the process in detail.

SPECIALIST SUPPLIERS

All About Framing
An ever expanding range of moulding, mount board and tools which can be ordered through their website at www.allaboutframing.com

Lion Picture Framing Supplies
Gilding supplies, Mighty Mounts, mini cable ties and compact disc holders can be ordered on their website at www.lionpic.co.uk

Rose and Hollis
Supply a large range of bare wood moulding in a variety of woods as well as some useful deep rebate mouldings. www.roseandhollis.co.uk

Simonart
Supply industrial framing equipment and are an examination centre for the Fine Art Trade Guild. www.djsimons.co.uk

Framers Equipment
Supply archival quality tapes, glue, polyester and more at www.framersequipment.co.uk/conservation.htm

Curtis Ward Art Materials
Supply gilding materials, artists' paint, liquid leaf at www.curtisward.com/Colour/Gilding

Pullingers Art Supplies
Supply gilding and artists' paints at www.pullingers.com

Ken Bromley
Art supplies, art masking gum.

Mighty Mounts
Phone: 785-234-3219
Toll Free: 1-800-255-0535
Fax: 888-255-2049
Bob Victor's, 1100 SE Rice Road, Topeka, KS 66607, USA.
E-mail: bob@bobvictors.com

INDEX